The Gratitude GAP

Transforming Leaders to Create More Human-Centric Workplaces

STAR SARGENT DARGIN

Printed in the United States of America, Pleasant Vines Publishing
ISBN: 978-0-9996972-1-4

What People Are Saying

Every so often, and not every day, a book comes along that articulates something we know in our gut but cannot say in words. Having the words brings that internal knowledge to life, gives us access to that inner wisdom, and changes how we see the world. When we see the world differently, the world sees us differently. Reducing the gratitude gap strengthens leadership effectiveness and encourages others to become better leaders by becoming better people. This book will change you and empower you to change others. ~ John D. Ela, CEO, Ela Management Group LLC, www.elamanagementgroup.com

*Too many leadership books focus on performance at the expense of people, leaving workplaces colder and trust in short supply. **The Gratitude Gap** offers a refreshing alternative - an honest, practical guide to leading with gratitude as the foundation for trust, connection, and results. Star Sargent Dargin shows why gratitude isn't soft or sentimental but a measurable leadership skill that transforms teams and cultures. Through stories, science, and tools, she helps leaders build workplaces where people feel seen, valued, and inspired to give their best. This book reminds us that gratitude isn't a luxury in leadership - it's the key to lasting success.* ~ Chris Kiklas, GVP and General Manager, UKG Ready

*I highly recommend this book to leaders, HR professionals, and anyone seeking growth in their personal or professional lives. **The Gratitude Gap** offers a powerful roadmap for embedding gratitude into daily life and leadership.* ~ Casey Hall, President, Casey Hall Training Associates, www.caseyhalltrainingassociates.com

Star Dargin has written an important guide to becoming a more thoughtful person and leader. I found the questions raised and examples presented meaningful challenges to how I think and act. Through the lens of gratitude comes a new alignment of words, actions, and options. As she notes: kindness and strength can coexist. Gratitude makes change possible in a positive and sustainable way. ~ Steve Kadish, Co-Author with Charlie Baker, Results: Getting Beyond Politics to Get Important Work Done

Research shows that practicing gratitude can improve leadership by enhancing decision-making, reducing burnout, and strengthening relationships. This book invites leaders to explore the impact of this often-overlooked skill. ~ Gwen Acton, PhD, author of Leadership for Scientists and Engineers, www.vivogroup.com

I learned a lot about gratitude from Star Dargin. Gratitude is good for business in every way. Leaders who express gratitude authentically can expect better customer relationships, more partnering opportunities, and improved employee retention. ~ Sandra Long, Author of LinkedIn for Personal Branding: The Ultimate Guide, www.postroadconsulting.com

The best leaders don't just drive results - they build trust. They know that people perform better when they feel seen, valued, and appreciated. This book provides the framework for leaders to add yet one more skill that will boost successful teams to achieve their goals. ~ Brian Proctor, Host of Tuesday's Thanks podcast and author of The Power of Gratitude at Work, www.powerofgratitudeatwork.com

The Gratitude Gap is a transformative guide for leaders who aim to create workplaces that are not only high-performing but deeply human. This book challenges the misconception that gratitude is merely a soft skill, redefining it as a core leadership competency that drives measurable results, strengthens relationships, and builds resilience.

Dargin introduces a clear and actionable Gratitude Practice Framework, supported by evidence-based research, practical tools, and real-world application strategies. Her use of relatable examples and compelling stories helps translate theory into everyday leadership practices.

Dargin provides a clear explanation—backed by research—on the benefits of gratitude in the workplace. Her book then provides a practical and "hit the ground running" approach to integrating gratitude into your skillset as a manager. ~ Kathleen Langone, PMP, author of The Miniature Painter Revealed, www.kathleenlangone.com

I learned a lot about gratitude from Star Dargin. Gratitude is good for business in every way. Leaders who express gratitude authentically can expect better customer relationships, more partnering opportunities, and improved employee retention. ~ Tara Whitney, Executive Coaching and CFO Advisory, www.whitebirchadvisory.com

Dedication

To you, and to the many who taught me the power of gratitude and how to cultivate it, no matter the circumstances. No ifs, ands, or buts. Mic Drop!

From you, I learned that gratitude makes life better. It can be strengthened. It can be easy or challenging. It's always worth it.

Contents

Chapter 1   Setting the Foundation 1

PART I   **The Gratitude Advantage** 13

Chapter 2   Invisible Performance Differentiator 15

Chapter 3   Science Proves Everything Is Better 25

PART II   **The Leadership Edge of Gratitude** 38

Chapter 4   What Leaders of the Future Need 40

Chapter 5   The Human Advantage 47

Chapter 6   Leadership, Vision, and Models 57

PART III   **The Paradox of Gratitude** 68

Chapter 7   Measure, Track, Grow 70

Chapter 8   Common Gratitude Challenges 80

Chapter 9   The Dark Side of Gratitude 88

PART IV   **Gratitude Breakthroughs** 97

Chapter 10   Definition Challenges 99

Chapter 11   Stress Buster Techniques 111

Chapter 12   Ted Leads with Gratitude 122

Chapter 13   I'm Fine, Toxic Positivity 133

Chapter 14   Confronting Negativity 143

Chapter 15   Forcing and Faking Gratitude 154

Chapter 16   Gratitude Translation Errors 164

Chapter 17   Redefining Giving 175

Chapter 18   Gratitude Limiting Beliefs 184

PART V   **Living the Gratitude Way** 193

Chapter 19 Gratitude Practice Framework 195

Chapter 20 Kitchen Sink Challenges.........................210

Chapter 21 Closing the Gratitude Gap......................227

Gratitude Leadership Questions 230

Gratitude and Thank You 232

Connect with Star 237

References for Each Chapter 240

Chapter 1
Setting the Foundation

As we express our gratitude, we must never forget that the highest appreciation is not to utter words, but to live by them.
~ John F. Kennedy

Over the years, I've learned two powerful lessons and discovered three truths about gratitude that every leader should know. These insights have shaped how I, and hundreds of other leaders, lead and live. When embraced and they become foundational, these ideas will transform your leadership, your workplace, and your life.

Lesson One: The Lie I Inherited
The first lesson starts with something my mother taught me. It was her mantra:

"If you can't say something nice, don't say anything at all." She meant well. She lived it, breathed it, and raised me on it. But when I stepped into leadership in the corporate world, I realized something important: That rule doesn't work in the real world.

And it especially doesn't work in leadership.

Early in my career, I avoided hard conversations. When things got tense, I stayed quiet and tried to be nice. Sometimes I ran away, rather than confronting injustices or speaking up. I even left my first job, a fun, fast-paced research and product development group with some of the world's best engineers. In that group, I worked on projects for legends like Stephen Hawking and Stevie Wonder, brilliant people without a traditional voice, which made me realize the power and limits of communication. Ironically, while working with people who couldn't speak, I was struggling to find *my* voice.

Over time, I saw the consequences of staying silent: things didn't get better, they got murky, unsafe, and, ironically, unkind.

I had to unlearn "being nice." And I had to learn how to say the difficult things in a kind, clear, and respectful way.

Lesson Two: Gratitude Is the Missing Ingredient
The second lesson? Gratitude is the missing foundation for *all* leadership success. Yes, all. Success, as defined here, is personal — it's whatever it means to *you*. It's about what matters most to you, your team, and your workplace. It's not necessarily about achievements, though they may be part of it.

I've read hundreds of leadership books, attended countless courses, and taught leadership in both university and corporate settings. But nearly all the models, techniques, tools, and frameworks I encountered were missing something vital: no foundation to build upon.

The gratitude gap is what is between what leadership is and what it can be when gratitude is strong and fully present.

Over the years, I have become a certified professional coach and worked with leaders across various industries. I've used, taught, and explored models like Situational Leadership, DISC (Dominance, Inspiring, Supportive, and Conscientiousness), StrengthsFinder, Emotional Intelligence, Radical Candor, and hundreds more. I learned Six Sigma from Motorola, taught project management based on PMI (Project Management Institute) standards, and completed a year-long, high-performance corporate leadership program that met on weekends.
Each experience had value.

But most of them overlooked something significant. Sometimes it was buried in jargon. Sometimes it was implied. Sometimes it was called something else, like recognition or appreciation. Occasionally, it got a passing mention.

What was missing? Gratitude.

Not the polite "thank you" kind, but the culture-shaping kind. The kind of gratitude that powers leadership – not as a soft skill, but as a foundation.

What I discovered was something far more powerful than any framework, leadership model, or system:

Gratitude. Real. Practiced. Foundational. Lived.
If You Want to Transform, Start by Closing the Gratitude Gap. If you want to become a better leader, more trusted, more effective, more human, start with gratitude. If you are already an experienced leader or grateful leader, strengthen your gratitude.

Science proves it. Experience confirms it. Leaders who practice gratitude shift teams, transform cultures, and achieve better results.

But here's the key: You have to move beyond merely believing in gratitude to living and leading with it.

Gratitude isn't just a feeling; it's a skill. A foundational system. A way of leading all the time, especially under pressure. It's easy to understand, but harder to sustain when there is uncertainty, the pace is fast, and the demands are high.

This book is for leaders who want to close that gap and build more human-centric workplaces through gratitude.

What's the Gratitude Gap?

Everyone has some gratitude. But most leaders:
- Don't treat it as a leadership skill
- Don't know their gratitude baseline
- Don't have a plan to strengthen it

Gratitude is like a Swiss Army Knife for leadership. It's compact, versatile, and powerful, always ready when you need it.

Conflict, change, uncertainty, burnout, pressure? Gratitude cuts through them all. It calms chaos. It builds clarity. It solves a wide range of problems and drives results. And it costs nothing.

Imagine a culture is calm, clear, and human, even in high-stress situations. Turnover is low. Innovation is high, and results are outstanding.

People feel seen, appreciated, and supported, not just for wins, but for effort, growth, and ideas.

A team where:
- Meetings aren't dreaded.
- People show up on time and are ready to contribute.
- Employees speak honestly, listen actively, and engage with purpose.
- Even the toughest issues, performance gaps, conflicts, and big changes are addressed head-on with openness and respect.

- Everyone is heard.

Compare that to the more common scene:
- Meetings that drag on with no resolution
- Gossip before and after, or worse, silence
- A few voices dominate while others are not heard from
- Real issues stay buried
- People are disengaged, underappreciated, and burned out

What's the difference? Gratitude.

Not the fluffy version. The practiced, embodied kind that is visible in how you lead, listen, learn, speak, and make decisions.

Three Gratitude Truths Every Leader Should Know
These three truths will guide this book and your journey to closing your gratitude gap.

Truth #1 - Everything is better with gratitude.
Gratitude improves performance, health, relationships, resilience, and clarity. It even accelerates physical recovery and burnout.

Truth #2 - Gratitude is a foundational leadership skill.
Gratitude is not a "nice-to-have." It's a multiplier. It makes every other tool: coaching, feedback, communication, more effective. It builds high-trust, high-performance cultures.

Truth #3 – Gratitude is both easy and challenging.
Gratitude is easy to express once. It's harder to sustain and practice daily, especially in chaos. Because it is a foundational skill, it involves learning new behaviors, habits, techniques, and frameworks that are specific to every leader and workplace. But that's where sustainable growth lives, and where leadership thrives.

Gratitude Doesn't Deny Reality, It Redefines It
Let's be clear: gratitude is not about being happy all the time; it doesn't sugarcoat, which can sometimes be mistaken for toxic positivity.

It doesn't ignore hardship, loss, or complexity.
It doesn't pretend bad behavior is acceptable.

Gratitude coexists with the hard stuff.
It helps us face it and move through it without losing our humanity.

What Gets in the Way?
Even the best leaders struggle with gratitude.

Not because they don't care, but because they're overwhelmed, busy, or focused on problems more than progress. It can be hard to stay grateful.

Gratitude doesn't just help us navigate today's challenges; it prepares us for a world that AI (Artificial Intelligence) is exponentially shaping.

AI, Gratitude, and the Human Advantage
AI can analyze data, write memos, conduct performance reviews, and even simulate empathy in customer service. That means leaders are no longer just being measured by what they know, but by how they show up as humans.

Here's the paradox:
The more we integrate AI into the workplace, the more human our leadership needs to become.

That's where gratitude comes in.
Gratitude can't be fully outsourced. You can automate a birthday reminder or a recognition email, but the impact of genuine, timely, leader-driven gratitude still carries more weight than any auto-generated message ever could.

As AI becomes more capable, what differentiates great leaders isn't speed or information; it's presence, empathy, and appreciation. Gratitude is the human advantage in an increasingly AI world.

Here's how gratitude helps leaders create human-centric workplaces and stand apart in the AI era:

- **Builds trust**, the machine can replicate trust, but it's not sustainable nor human
- **Creates human connections**, especially in remote teams
- **Keeps the focus on the human purpose and values** in the chaos of change

- **Keeps leaders grounded** and emotionally intelligent

We can let AI handle many things, like repetitive tasks. As leaders, we need to double down on the irreplaceable humanness, and gratitude is at the top of that list. Gratitude is how we bring a more human-centric workplace to life.

That's what this book will help with: sharing over 50+ challenges that block gratitude and giving you tools to overcome them.

Because when gratitude is strong, results come faster. And people follow leaders who lead with it.

This is not a Self-Help Book. I'm not a therapist. I'm not a gratitude guru.

I'm a former computer science major and corporate leader who slowly transitioned to become a self-employed speaker and leadership coach over twenty years ago. Yes, this book is my legacy, and I want to give back to the world what I think it needs: understanding, connection, and more humanity. I believe gratitude is the foundation for that.

Gratitude is for everyone, and when leaders close the gap and strengthen it, the impact is multiplied exponentially. And I've seen what happens when leaders treat gratitude like the strategic skill it is.

The challenges and solutions I've identified come from many places. I've interviewed consultants, researchers, hotel managers, stylists, and more. I've seen gratitude save a family, shift a mindset, and ground leaders during times of tragedy.

I once spoke with a hotel manager who had to call the next of kin for guests after a mass shooting. It was gut-wrenching. What struck them was this: the people who found something, anything, to be grateful for, even during unimaginable grief, were the ones who moved forward with more strength. Gratitude didn't erase the pain, but it helped people keep going.

Gratitude doesn't prevent hardship.

But it *does* keep us from being consumed by it.

Start Now and Where You Are

This is a book for leaders. Gratitude is for everyone. Leaders shape others and help others be better. Leaders impact the world, and how they lead can be transformational. This book will help you, the leader, cultivate and strengthen your gratitude. For you, your workplace, and the world. I hope to achieve this through stories, science, and practical tools that you can use every day.

You already have a gratitude baseline to start from.

Gratitude is not soft. It's strong. It's not a detour. It's the foundation. When leaders lead with gratitude, it spreads. It sticks. And it transforms.

Setting the Foundation Takeaways

At the end of each chapter is a summary of the main points called Takeaways. Followed by three reflection questions for you to ponder and answer that collectively will help you identify your unique gratitude challenges and strengthen your gratitude. Additionally, in the back, there is a more comprehensive list of references to support each chapter.

- Truth #1 – Everything is Better with Gratitude
- Truth #2 – Gratitude is a Foundational Leadership Skill
- Truth #3 – Gratitude is Easy and Challenging
- Lesson One – Be Kind, Not Nice
- Lesson Two – Gratitude is the Missing Ingredient for Leadership Models

Reflection Questions

1. Where do you see a gap between your belief in gratitude and your leadership behaviors?

2. What early messages about gratitude or "being nice" shaped your leadership communication style?

3. How does your team currently experience gratitude from you in the workplace? Is it consistent, situational, or rare?

PART I
The Gratitude Advantage
Why gratitude transforms everything.

Truth #1: Everything Is Better with Gratitude
This part reveals how gratitude acts as an invisible performance differentiator, weaving science and stories together to show that when leaders intentionally close the gratitude gap, workplaces thrive and results soar.
Gratitude turns what we have into enough, and more.
~ Melody Beattie

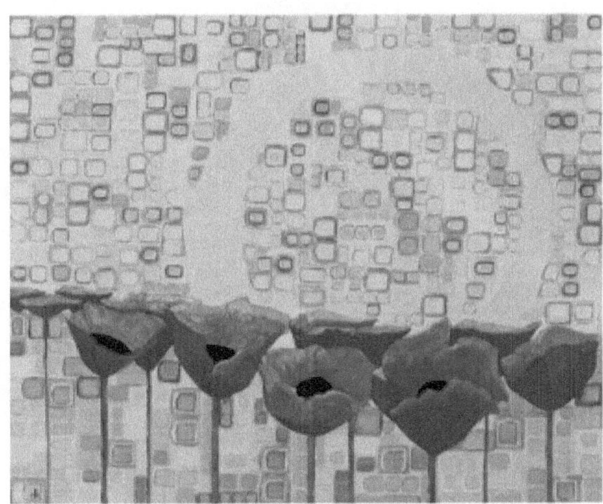

Enough Sun for Us All

Chapter 2
Invisible Performance Differentiator

Gratitude is not just a switch to turn on when things go well but also a light that shines in the darkness.
~ Dr. Robert Emmons, Gratitude Researcher

Let's start with something that might sting a little:

Most leaders are probably misusing or underusing gratitude right now, without even realizing it. Even in the smallest ways, this disconnect is holding back your results, your team, and your leadership potential. If you want to improve almost any situation: conflict, stress, change, or challenge, you must first embrace gratitude and close the gap.

Truth #1: Everything is better with gratitude.
Gratitude isn't just a soft feeling or a Hallmark moment. It's one of the easiest ways to stay grounded in a world that is not all sunshine and unicorns.

Even before we had science to prove the power of gratitude, we had the wisdom. The Roman philosopher Cicero called gratitude *the parent of all virtues*. Positive Psychology research backs that up. According to the VIA Institute on Character, gratitude is a core strength, and they say that when you understand and strengthen your character, you can thrive.

What Gratitude Improves in Leadership

Leaders who cultivate strong, intentional gratitude see improvements in nearly every area of their team and business lives. They see results such as:

- Lower stress, anxiety, and negativity
- More calm, clarity, and resilience
- Higher employee engagement and retention
- Greater innovation and creativity
- Better decision-making and collaboration
- Stronger, more human-centric cultures
- Higher-performing teams
- Improved business outcomes

If that list sounds idealistic, it's not. It's research-backed, and it's exactly what strong gratitude makes possible. Check out the many references at the end of the book that support those statements. When you believe in truth #1, that gratitude makes everything better, and then you learn truth #2, that gratitude is a skill that strengthens it, you'll experience the power of gratitude.

The "Grateful Enough" Myth and Challenge

The most common myth and challenge I see in leadership?

Believing you are already "grateful enough."
This is the eye-roll moment. The part where some leaders mentally check out and think, "I already do this. There is nothing new to learn here." That is a myth.

Here's the thing: you can never be too grateful, because the moment you stop actively practicing it, the benefits stall. Gratitude is not a checkbox. It's a skill that can be strengthened over time.

Leaders get stalled because of dozens of hidden barriers:
- They don't see gratitude as a strategic skill and don't work to strengthen it
- They believe it's too "soft" for tough leadership moments
- They've never identified their own unique gratitude challenges

Some challenges are obvious, like how to stay grateful around negative people. Others are more subtle and complex, like working in cultures steeped in toxic positivity, where "gratitude" is code for "just get over it."
And because gratitude is often invisible, misunderstood, and deeply personal, it's easy to assume we're grateful enough … when we're just scratching the surface.

Unless you've mastered gratitude, like Desmond Tutu (a Peace Activist), Malala (a Nobel Peace Prize winner), or Yoda (Star Wars, fictional sage, gratitude he teaches), chances are there's room to grow.

Misunderstood and Changes Meaning Over Time

Ask twenty people to define gratitude, and you'll get twenty answers. Is it a feeling? A belief? A behavior? Is it a virtue? A leadership trait? A cultural practice? Yes, No, and It depends.

The definition has evolved over the centuries, and even today's popular dictionaries define gratitude differently and vastly differently from

GRATITUDE, noun

[Latin *gratitudo*, from gratus, pleasing. See Grace.]

An emotion of the heart, excited by a favor or benefit received; a sentiment of kindness or goodwill towar a benefactor; thankfulness.
Gratitude is an agreeable emotion, consisting in or accompanided with goodwill to a benefactor, and a disposition to make a suitable return of benefits or services, or when no return can be made, with a desire to see the benefactor prosperous and happy.
Gratitude is a virtue of the highest excellence, as it implies a feeling and a generous heart, and a proper sense of duty.

the 1828 dictionary definition shown here. In the early centuries, gratitude was more about duty, reciprocity, and moral obligation, to God, to lords, to benefactors.
Gratitude has been called all of those things—and more. It has been a part of every major religion, every ancient culture, and modern psychological theory. But because it's so universal, it's also hard to pin down.

And in the workplace? It gets even messier.

Sometimes it shows up as recognition. At other times, as a gesture of appreciation or praise. And sometimes it's completely absent, disguised by compensation, titles, or passive-aggressive thank-you's.

Add cultural, generational, and personality differences, and confusion grows fast. What feels like gratitude to one person might feel forced, fake, or even offensive to another. Examples of gratitude gone wrong include sarcasm in tone when giving praise, thanks spoken to the all-mighty "we," or gratitude offered where it is undeserved.

A generational difference is that Boomers may see gratitude as a formal thank-you, while Gen Z might expect ongoing acknowledgment and reciprocity.

Leaders have asked me:
"Why should I thank people for doing their job? That's what they're paid for."
Sadly, too many times, people have told me:
"I left my last role because I didn't feel appreciated at all."
This is the result of having a gratitude gap.

Gratitude Is Invisible (But Measurable)
Gratitude is hard to see. You *feel* it, but it's not always obvious to others.

Some organizations mandate gratitude, daily emails, "thank you" quotas, or awkward icebreakers. Most of these backfire because they come off as performative, not authentic.

If you want gratitude to work in your organization, it needs to be:
- **Visible** (spoken, shown, or felt)
- **Personalized** (not templated)
- **Measured and intentional** (like any good leadership practice)

- **Integrated and incorporated** (part of processes, structures, visions, strategies)

Later in this book, you'll get a tool to assess your gratitude baseline, so you can track your progress, just like you would any other leadership goal.

Gratitude Builds Self-Awareness and Brand
Here's a powerful leadership insight:
What you're grateful for says a lot about who you are.
When you say out loud what you appreciate, you're also revealing what you don't appreciate.

Examples:
- "I appreciate this team's support." (Implied: I don't like teams that don't support each other.)
- "I'm grateful for my peers who make me laugh." (Implied: I value lightness and notice when it's missing.)
- "I appreciate people who help me find answers." (Implied: I get frustrated when people don't collaborate.)

These aren't bad. In fact, they build clarity and trust. Gratitude, when expressed sincerely, makes your leadership brand visible. What you value becomes real and specific. It helps people understand how you think, what matters to you, and how to work with you.

That's what I mean when I say gratitude shapes executive presence. It doesn't just reflect who you are, it reveals you.

Gratitude Requires Holding Opposites

Real gratitude isn't blind. It doesn't ignore the hard stuff; it coexists with it. This is where many leaders get stuck. They think they can only be grateful when things are good. But authentic gratitude lives in the "AND".

- I'm in pain AND I'm grateful for the care I'm receiving.
- I'm frustrated with my team AND I'm grateful for their effort.
- I'm grieving AND I'm grateful for the memories.

Holding opposites is uncomfortable, nuanced, and can be hard to do. It's easier to pick a side.

But strong leaders don't flinch. They practice the skill of holding tension between what's wrong and what's working. This is emotional maturity. And gratitude helps build it.

Gratitude Has Depth

Gratitude isn't always a bright flash of joy. Sometimes it's a quiet sense of strength. Sometimes it lasts two seconds. Other times, it stays with you for days or a lifetime.

Wendy, former Chief of Culture at New Level Work and an active executive coach, as well as a long-time gratitude practitioner, shared with me a story about a time when she felt deep gratitude in every cell of her body. She found herself driving across Boston on her way to a second round of testing after receiving a diagnosis of cancer minutes before.

Wendy knew she easily could have collapsed in sadness and fear, as many would. Instead, she remained hopeful and present, repeatedly asking herself what she was grateful for. She found so many things: the sunny day, the helpful nurses, and the easy drive. When Wendy arrived for her testing, she was smiling, laughing, and hopeful. She was amazed at how gratitude changed her on that short car ride and attributes that to her strong gratitude. She fully recovered. The experience stuck with her as a profound reminder of what gratitude can do, even in crisis.

Gratitude Drives Business Results

Plenty of research shows what some leaders now accept as fact: that positive, supportive cultures outperform.

For example, according to Gallup, analysis of over 183,000 business units in companies with high employee engagement, fueled by appreciation, outperforms peers by 23% in profitability.

Teams with strong emotional health, fueled by psychological safety and appreciation, innovate more, engage more, and stay longer. That translates directly to the bottom line.

My personal and unscientific but fun example:
A family member of mine began investing in companies I've highlighted and researched for their gratitude-based cultures. Five years later, those are the top-performing stocks in their portfolio of 50+ stocks.

Gratitude and the AI Era

Artificial Intelligence is reshaping leadership. It can write reports, analyze data, and even simulate empathy. But what it *can't* do is be *you*, a real, human, vulnerable, trusted leader.

As AI grows, the real value of leadership will be how human you are. And that's where gratitude becomes a differentiator.
- It builds human trust.
- It creates connections across cultures and remote teams.
- It anchors values in the face of change.
- It keeps leaders emotionally grounded.

The best leaders won't compete with AI; they'll focus on what makes them irreplaceable. Gratitude is the human advantage in an AI-driven world.

This first truth lays the foundation. The next two reveal why gratitude is so often neglected, and how to make it a sustainable part of your leadership.

Invisible Performance Differentiator Takeaways
- Gratitude Truth #1: Everything is better with gratitude.
- Gratitude improves health, engagement, innovation, and results.
- Thinking you're "grateful enough" is a common gratitude challenge.
- Gratitude is complex, misunderstood, and often invisible.
- Gratitude reveals your values and strengthens your leadership presence.
- Gratitude improves business results.
- Strong gratitude requires emotional nuance, especially holding opposites.
- In an AI-powered world, gratitude sets human leaders apart.

Reflection Questions
1. Who do you consider a "gratitude expert," and why?

2. Describe a time you saw gratitude change a situation or team dynamic.

3. What challenges do you see for building your own and your workplace's gratitude?

Chapter 3
Science Proves Everything Is Better

People don't know what they don't know, especially about gratitude, which is why we need to keep passing it on.
~ Wendy Hanson, former VP of Culture at Better Manager

Most people don't understand how airplanes work, but we still board them and trust they'll get us safely to our destination. We trust the engineers, the systems, and the science behind them. Gratitude is similar. We don't need to fully understand every mechanism to know it works. The first step is belief. The second is practice.

Unlike aviation, though, there are no federal regulations or checklists for gratitude. No one makes you practice it. Gratitude is yours to build, strengthen, and sustain on your own. And if you're skeptical, science has a lot to say that might convince you.

This chapter is your glimpse into that research, revealing how and why gratitude works in your brain, body, and leadership.

Experts Ziglar, Huberman, Emmons, and Seligman
Each of these experts comes from a different angle – sales, neuroscience, and psychology – but they converge on one truth: gratitude works.

Before science proved it, Zig Ziglar, a salesman, motivational speaker, and author from the 1970s, said, "Gratitude is the healthiest of all human emotions. The more you express gratitude for what you have, the more likely you will have even more to express gratitude for."

Andrew Huberman, PhD, neuroscientist and Stanford professor, translates gratitude-related brain science into practical advice. He emphasizes that gratitude doesn't just feel good; it creates long-term neural shifts and physiological benefits. His work is especially popular with high-performing professionals and biohackers.

Robert Emmons, PhD, professor of psychology at UC Davis and one of the world's leading gratitude researchers, has shown in numerous studies that gratitude increases happiness and reduces depression, stress, envy, and regret. His work forms the scientific backbone of the field.

Martin Seligman, often referred to as the father of positive psychology, helped define gratitude as a core value of human flourishing. His work emphasizes that gratitude isn't fluff; it's functional, strategic, and measurable.

The science of gratitude, rooted in both neuroscience and social science, is growing exponentially. In 2024, I conducted a quick search on Science Direct, www.sciencedirect.com, and found nearly 70,000 research articles on gratitude. Why so many? *Because gratitude improves almost everything.* Now we will dig into the *why*. Here's what the science says is actually happening in your body and brain and why it matters for leaders.

Improves Physical, Mental, and Social Health
Because the benefits are so wide-reaching across multiple fields of study, I'm simplifying the benefits that science has proven by categorizing them into these three overarching and overlapping categories:

Physical Health	Mental Health	Social Health
Better sleep	More happiness	Stronger relationships
Stronger immunity	Less anxiety and depression	Higher emotional inteligence
Less pain and inflammation	Greater resilience	More empathy and generosity
Lower blood pressure	Higher self-esteem	
Fewer sick days	Increased mental clarity	

Imagine if everyone in your workplace were even slightly better in each of these areas. That's the multiplying power of gratitude.

What this means for you as a leader is that when you strengthen your own gratitude, you raise the baseline for everyone around you, one conversation, decision, and moment at a time.

My Ankle, My Brain, and My Realization

After I broke my ankle in 2016, I experienced firsthand how gratitude supported my healing. Experiencing the transformation of gratitude led me to research and discover just how deeply gratitude affects us. I was able to verify through science that my experiences of shifting my leadership and physically healing my ankle were related to and correlated with when I first started practicing gratitude in the early 2000s.

Gratitude and the Brain

When you feel gratitude, your brain literally lights up. Think of it as a movie studio, the core team is:

Thalamus = the director of photography, capturing sensory input and sending it where it needs to go.

Amygdala = the drama editor, deciding if something is emotionally intense or potentially dangerous, often before you're fully aware.

Neocortex = the screenwriter and producer, crafting meaning and deciding how to respond; its medial prefrontal cortex (mPFC) is especially active during self-reflection, empathy, and gratitude

Together, they process experience in milliseconds. Gratitude helps the "crew" frame calmer, clearer stories, especially when paired with the feel-good chemicals dopamine, oxytocin, serotonin, and endorphins.

Your Emotional Soundtrack
Gratitude floods the brain with feel-good chemicals that boost motivation, connection, and calmness:
Dopamine - the motivation molecule, rewarding what feels good.
Oxytocin - the bonding chemical, building trust and connection.
Serotonin - the mood stabilizer, creating a sense of calm and satisfaction.
Endorphins - the body's natural painkillers, easing tension and amplifying joy.

Working together, they keep you resilient under pressure, and gratitude is one of the most sustainable ways to activate them. It doesn't just make you feel good; it rewires your "movie studio" to tell better stories. These chemicals constantly shift in response to stress, hormones, trauma, past experiences, and more, sometimes from clear triggers like praise, other times from vague cues you hardly notice.

THE CORE TEAM
(AND THE FOUR FEEL-GOOD CHEMICALS)

The Core Team

Thalamus = the director of photography
It captures incoming sensory information

Amygdala = the drama editor
It detects emotional intensity

Neocortex = the screenwriter and producer
It crafts the story — mPFC = empathy editor

- Self-reflection
- Empathy
- Perspective-taking

- Self-reflection
- Empathy
- Perspective-taking

The Four Feel-Good Chemicals

Dopamine the motivation molecule It rewards what feels good	**Oxytocin** the bonding chemical It builds trust and connection
	Serotonin the mood stabilizer It regulates emotion
	Endorphins the body's natural painkillers They amplify joy

Gratitude rewires your inner film core team. Your thalamus frames the shot. Your amygdala reacts to the drama. Your neocortex writes the next scene. And gratitude adds light, warmth, and a killer soundtrack.

What this means for you as a leader is that when you practice gratitude, you're not just changing how you feel; you're changing how you lead, respond, and create culture in real time.

Gratitude and the "Fight or Flight" Response

When we feel threatened, the amygdala hijacks our emotions, triggering a response that pushes us into survival mode. Traditionally known as "fight or flight," this response has evolved to include other "F" behaviors, such as freeze, fawn, and faint. In these states, our decision-making narrows, zeroing in on only the threat. We react. We protect. We shut down. It's our amygdala that creates this reaction.

The key insight is this: our bodies often treat workplace tension the same way they would a predator attack. When you are criticized, your amygdala responds. You may unconsciously tense up, tighten your fists, and your breathing may become shallow. This response is ancient and automatic. But it's not always helpful or relevant. Rarely is a perceived threat in a meeting life or death.

The good news is that, as humans, we can rewire our automatic responses. Thanks to the neocortex, especially the medial prefrontal cortex, when notified of a potential threat, we can learn how to respond differently.

Practicing gratitude strengthens the connection between the prefrontal cortex and the amygdala, helping you respond rather than react, regulate your emotions more effectively, and lower baseline stress levels.

Studies (including fMRI research) show that gratitude reduces amygdala reactivity and activates the prefrontal cortex, especially areas related to empathy and social reasoning.

The more gratitude we have, the easier it is to discern what the best course of action is. Gratitude doesn't erase the threat; instead, it creates enough psychological distance for discernment. It seems like the moment has slowed down, helping you choose your response. You might take a breath, speak up calmly, or even stay present instead of fleeing or fighting.

Over time, practicing gratitude rewires the brain, allowing for calmer, more open responses to occur unconsciously. The rewiring process is called neuroplasticity. Neuroplasticity is like water forming a stream; your thoughts carve new pathways. With repetition, gratitude becomes your default.

What this means for you as a leader is that you can rewire your stress response. So instead of reacting on autopilot, you'll respond with clarity, calm, and intention.

Gratitude is not a light switch you flip on and off. It's more like a drip, a steady, sustaining presence that shapes your reactions over time. You build it slowly. You maintain it deliberately.

Not All Feel-Good Chemicals Are Equal
Gratitude isn't the only way to boost feel-good chemicals. Exercise, sunshine, prayer, meditation, and breathwork can help, too. But less healthy triggers. Like alcohol, sugar, online shopping, doom-scrolling, and certain video games and ads often manipulate these chemicals for short-term effect and long-term harm.

Take Candy Crush or a Super Bowl ad. Both are intentionally designed to spike dopamine (and sometimes serotonin) to keep your attention and leave you feeling good about something, whether from a puzzle win or a product you've never tried. In 2024, a 30-second Super Bowl spot cost over $7 million for exactly this reason: advertisers know how to hijack your feel-good chemistry.

The difference? Gratitude activates the same chemicals naturally, without addiction, manipulation, or side effects. It's sustainable, authentic, self-generated, and within your control.

And the benefits go beyond mood. One study published in *BMC Psychology* found that people with higher levels of gratitude were significantly less likely to develop addictive behaviors like online gaming.

Gratitude seems to support healthier coping strategies, helping people seek social support instead of emotional escape.

What this means for you as a leader is that the more you model sustainable emotional health, the more your team will follow suit, and gratitude is one of the simplest ways to start.

Mirror Neurons, Gratitude Is Contagious

One of the most fascinating discoveries in neuroscience is the role of mirror neurons. These brain cells fire not only when you experience something, but when you observe someone else experiencing it. Mirror neurons are most activated when interacting with others in person.

That's why yawns and smiles are contagious. Gratitude works the same way. When a leader expresses real gratitude, others feel it. Their brains light up. Their body chemistry shifts. Think of gratitude like Bluetooth: when yours is activated, others can pick up the signal. This is leadership at its most human and influential. This is why gratitude isn't just personal, it's cultural. It spreads.

What this means for you as a leader is that your gratitude doesn't stop with you; it spreads. The more consistently and authentically you express it, the more you shift the emotional tone of your team and culture.

Real vs. Fake Gratitude

Can you fake gratitude? Kind of. Sometimes people try to appear grateful by thinking about something unrelated (e.g., "I'm thankful for my dog.") to conjure an emotional tone before giving insincere thanks. The result may sound genuine, but people, especially your team, can often tell when it's not real.

Gratitude that isn't authentic can backfire. Trust erodes. The message is lost. That's why your tone, body language, and timing can matter more than your words. Authentic gratitude shows up in all three.

Written gratitude, video messages, and emails often lack tone, timing, and body language, making it difficult to discern the true meaning. It's more easily misunderstood. In-person expressions are most effective for expressing gratitude.

And whether it's real or performative often depends on something deeper: your personal gratitude baseline.

Your Gratitude Baseline

Science shows that your gratitude levels are fluid, changing microsecond by microsecond, day by day, and over the years. They change depending on a multitude of factors. Where you start is based on your biology, experiences, culture, personality, and situation. Where you are now depends on how much you commit to and practice strengthening.

Sadly, for some people, it's not until a trauma, a life-threatening experience, or aging that they turn to gratitude as a way of life. The good news is that we know you can proactively build it now, on your own terms.

This is why Truth #1 matters: Gratitude makes everything better. When gratitude becomes a consistent practice, it transforms your health, mindset, and leadership impact.

What this means for you as a leader is that your gratitude doesn't have to be perfect, just real, consistent, and practiced with intention. That's how transformation begins.

Science Proves Everything is Better Takeaways
- Belief is the first step. Practice is the second.
- Gratitude improves physical, mental, and social health.
- Gratitude regulates feel-good brain chemicals and calms stress responses.
- Gratitude is like a drip, slow, steady, and sustaining.
- Mirror neurons make gratitude contagious.
- Real gratitude builds trust; fake gratitude erodes it.
- You can build your gratitude baseline at any age, in any season.

Reflection Questions
1. What do you currently believe about the science of gratitude? Does that belief help or hinder your ability to practice it?

2. Which aspect of gratitude science do you want to explore further?

3. How can you become more aware and spread the contagious effect of gratitude in your team or workplace?

PART II
The Leadership Edge of Gratitude
Building human-centric leadership skills

Truth #2: Gratitude Is a Leadership Skill
Here you'll discover why gratitude is not just being nice, but rather, a foundational leadership skill, essential for navigating change, shaping vision, and leading in an AI-driven, ever-shifting future.

Silent gratitude isn't much use to anyone.
~ G.B. Stern, Author

We are all in this together

Chapter 4
What Leaders of the Future Need

Gratitude is a skill you should get an A+ in.
~ Marshall Goldsmith, New York Times bestselling
author and executive coach

Without gratitude, workplaces can easily become thankless, fearful, and gossip-driven environments. Turnover rises, engagement falls, and performance suffers. On the other hand, leaders who intentionally practice gratitude cultivate human-centric cultures that are innovative, collaborative, resilient, and ready for change. These leaders are open to change and more capable of handling challenges because they aren't stuck in a state of survival mode, fight, flight, freeze, or fawn. Gratitude isn't just a nicety; it's a leadership strategy.

We now understand that leadership is both born and made. Historically, people believed leadership was inherited or innate. But today, science and experience tell a different story: leadership can be

learned. That's why billions of dollars are spent globally on leadership development.
In 2023, Fortune Business Insights valued the leadership training market at $33.9 billion, with rapid growth projected.

Leadership coaching is also surging. According to the International Coach Federation (ICF), there were more than 122,974 coach practitioners globally in 2025. In the United States alone, the coaching industry generated $5.34 billion USD in 2025, nearly doubling its 2023 revenue of $2.849 billion.

Coaching now represents a $20 billion market and delivers some of the highest returns on investment, 500% to 788% ROI, according to multiple studies.

So, with all this investment—billions spent each year—what are organizations actually trying to develop? It comes down to one essential question: What do leaders really need to thrive now?

Gratitude, it turns out, cuts across all industries and leadership levels. It's foundational to almost every leadership competency and outcome.

The Skills Leaders Need
Today's leaders face fast-moving, volatile environments. Much of it is driven by AI, but not all of

it. Analysts, researchers, and leadership thinkers agree that modern leaders must:
- Lead through constant change (VUCA: Volatility, Uncertainty, Complexity, Ambiguity)
- Build human connection and authenticity, especially in an AI-powered world
- Operate ethically and morally

And to do that, they need skills like:
- Resilience and adaptability
- Innovation and creativity
- Empathy and emotional intelligence
- Clear communication and strategic execution
- A growth mindset

Organizational psychologist and bestselling author Adam Grant says it this way: "In the past, people were hired and promoted based on ability. In the future, the more valuable currency will be agility."

Daniel Lamarre, former CEO of Cirque du Soleil, infused gratitude into his leadership even if he didn't always call it that. In his book *Balancing Acts*, gratitude is quietly present in his decisions, tone, and philosophy. That's what makes gratitude powerful; it's so deeply ingrained in great leadership that it can be easy to miss.

Gratitude is a strategic skill. It amplifies everything else.

Leaders Who Lead with Gratitude

The most effective leaders I coach already have a gratitude foundation. They're curious, open to feedback, and committed to growth even when they're in crisis.

I've seen leaders go from venting and defending to visioning and solving. And the pivot usually starts with a shift to gratitude. Sometimes it takes an hour of unloading before I see their posture change or tone soften. Other times, one powerful question, like, "What did you appreciate about that?" shifts them into gratitude.

Recently, a leader I coached over a decade ago reconnected, and I asked her what she remembered about our coaching. She didn't remember much about the coaching or the tools we used. What stuck with her? The shift to gratitude. Back then, she'd been consumed by fear, worried about losing her job, overwhelmed by conflict. Once she accessed gratitude, she saw the situation clearly and started making empowered choices. Today, she's thriving in a C-suite role at a tech company. She's confident, courageous, and having fun.

That's the power of gratitude. It shifts people from fear to freedom by interrupting survival mode and opening space for choice.

What this means for you as a leader is that gratitude isn't optional or extra. It's essential, especially when navigating change, coaching others, or influencing culture from the top down.

Gratitude: Fund It and Budget It!
"If you want a recognition program to succeed," says Brian Proctor, the author of *The Power of Gratitude at Work*, "you have to design it like any strategic initiative, plan it, communicate it, and get buy-in."

The same is true for gratitude. If it's going to transform your leadership, it can't be left to chance. It has to be *taught, modeled,* and *budgeted*, just like any core competency.

If we know gratitude fuels better performance, why aren't we training it like every other leadership skill?

Gratitude programs and training should be:
- Budgeted and funded
- Built into leadership development plans
- Embedded into team practices and organizational culture
- Scaled for senior leaders who influence large systems

There are three areas to cover in gratitude training:
1. Gratitude tools for individual leaders
2. Creating cultures of appreciation and recognition

3. Advanced practice for overcoming gratitude challenges

Every level of leadership can incorporate gratitude. Team leaders can start meetings with real appreciation. Senior leaders can create ways to measure and incorporate gratitude processes. All leaders can evaluate how their gratitude is communicated and perceived by others.

And when gratitude is embedded in coaching or leadership development, the results tend to be even stronger, because gratitude fuels mindset shifts that lead to lasting change.

The most successful leaders I know speak openly about their appreciation, reflect on it regularly, and use it to guide decision-making. They don't just feel it, they make it visible and contagious.

What Leaders of the Future Need Takeaways

- Gratitude is a foundational skill; it creates the conditions for lasting transformation, not just performance improvements.
- Gratitude is a strategic, learnable leadership skill.
- Leadership development is a massive, fast-growing industry, with coaching ROI consistently outperforming training.
- Leaders must operate in VUCA environments and demonstrate humanity, adaptability, and moral clarity.
- Gratitude supports and strengthens all other key leadership traits.
- Senior leaders must ensure their appreciation is felt as authentic and equitable.
- Gratitude training can happen at the individual, team, and organizational levels.

Reflection Questions

1. What essential skills do you, as a leader, need right now, and how does gratitude support them?

2. What processes or habits around appreciation could improve your team or culture?

3. How can you help someone shift to gratitude, especially in challenging moments?

Chapter 5
The Human Advantage

In an age of ubiquitous AI, what does it mean to be human?

Today's leaders are navigating relentless change from global disruptions like AI and climate threats to everyday stressors like overflowing inboxes and shifting family dynamics. Gratitude doesn't make change disappear, but it does make it manageable. It helps leaders stay grounded when things feel uncertain or out of control. Leaders who pair change with gratitude move faster, with less stress and more sustainability. They lead from intention, not reaction.

What this means for you as a leader is that if you want to lead change effectively, gratitude helps you stay grounded and intentional rather than reactive.

When the World Changed: COVID-19
The COVID-19 pandemic was a global masterclass in change. None of us escaped unscathed. According to the World Health Organization (WHO), anxiety and

depression rates surged 25% in the pandemic's first year. Yet, the people who weathered the storm best often had one thing in common: a strong gratitude practice.

Gratitude didn't erase the fear, grief, or confusion. But it helped people focus on what mattered most: staying connected to others and accessing inner strength during uncertain times. The pandemic also forced organizations to change quickly. Remote work, virtual collaboration, and redefined priorities became the new normal. Many people re-evaluated their lives and careers. The Great Resignation of 2022 saw over 50 million Americans quit their jobs in search of meaning, balance, and a better quality of life.

Change on that scale doesn't just happen. There were numerous examples of both poorly led and well-led changes throughout the COVID-19 pandemic. And it's more successful when led with gratitude.

What this means for you as a leader is that the next time you're facing change, start by asking: "What am I grateful for right now?" It's not fluff. It's focus.

Enter AI: The Next Wave of Change

Now we're facing a transformation that's moving faster than anything before, and redefining what it means to lead.

Artificial Intelligence is no longer a buzzword; it's here. And it's changing everything.

Some people fear AI will take away jobs, create inequality, or even threaten humanity itself. Others see it as a tool for innovation and efficiency. The truth? It's all of that and more. AI is moving faster than any previous major technology shift. According to PwC, AI could contribute up to $15.7 trillion to the global economy by 2030. Statista reports that AI funding more than doubled to $66.8 billion in 2021 alone.

The pace of change is staggering, and today's leaders must rise to meet it with clarity and courage.

What this means for you as a leader is that you can't control the speed of AI, but you can control how you respond, and gratitude helps you respond with clarity, not fear.

From Sci-Fi Fan to AI Technologist: A Personal Perspective on Change

Since childhood, I've always loved reading dystopian, apocalyptic, and science fiction stories that explore the blurred lines between technology and humanity. That love for sci-fi is partly why AI both excites and unnerves me. In May 2023, a group of AI experts signed an open letter warning that AI posed an extinction-level threat, on par with nuclear war and pandemics. That was a chilling moment, even for a lifelong sci-fi fan. I keep wanting to remind everyone of the three laws of Robotics by Isaac Asimov, which basically state that robots (AI) can't harm humans.

I've seen these patterns before, as a technologist in the early days of the PC era. I was in the trenches during the PC/Networking wars as a PC networking engineering leader at a hardware company. The lack of standardization caused undue chaos: Which hardware, operating system, cables, and connectors do we use, and which will become standards? What apps will survive, and for how long? I worked on technologies that have mostly faded into the sunset, such as Digital Equipment Corporation's PDP-11s, the operating system OS/2, the spreadsheet Lotus 123, computer text-to-speech, speech recognition, the search engine Alta Vista, and the Internet browser Mosaic. Ironically, the speech recognition algorithm developed in the 1980s by Dr. Dennis Klatt is still around in different forms. It was the voice of Stephen Hawking and Carlos, the quirky sidekick of the famous Boston DJ Charles Laquidara.

AI is following a similar arc, but faster, broader, and more visible. According to the AI experts from my favorite podcast, *Last Week in AI*, one month of AI growth is like ten years of any other technology. As one AI VP of Technology and Engineering told me, "AI is debilitating and eliminating in contrast to previous revolutions. It has the potential to replace core human capabilities like the brain and soul, creating a stark divide between the 'haves' and 'have-nots'. Not everybody will get a choice. That is why leaders MUST step up and responsibly manage AI."

This isn't science fiction. AI is already writing obituaries for the deceased and funeral speeches for grieving families. It's also being used in hospitals and birth centers to help monitor patient risk factors and suggest treatment options, guiding care from the very beginning of life to the very end. Everyone is born, and everyone eventually dies; these are two universal truths, and AI is now involved in both. Whether it's a funeral speech or a medical diagnosis, a marketing campaign or a business strategy, AI is touching nearly every part of human life, and it's just getting started. It's not a question of if leaders will be impacted; it's when. And how they respond.

What this means for you as a leader is that the more AI reshapes how we work, the more valuable your distinctly human leadership becomes.

Why Gratitude Matters in the Age of AI

AI can simulate many things. It isn't grateful, but it can simulate gratitude. AI can't trust, but it can build people's trust. It can't replace the human touch that comes from authentic leadership. In a world increasingly shaped by algorithms, the most powerful differentiator for leaders is how human they are.

Gratitude is the anchor

It keeps leaders centered in the midst of massive transformation. It opens the door to curiosity instead of fear. It fosters connection across generational, cultural, and technological divides. And it keeps us grounded in our values when speed and uncertainty threaten to knock us off course.

I know this firsthand. In the first drafts of this book, I used AI minimally, mostly for research. As the writing progressed and years went by, I found myself using AI tools more frequently to help shape ideas, clarify the structure, and serve as an idea partner. The voice, experiences, and insights are all mine, but AI helped me organize and refine them. Ironically, when I asked multiple AI tools about gratitude, they often acknowledged its value but couldn't agree on how to define it or apply it. Even AI struggles with gratitude.

What this means for you as a leader is that your ability to understand and express authentic gratitude is one of the most irreplaceable things about you.

Gratitude Makes Change Easier

Leadership is the art of guiding people through change. And gratitude is one of the most effective tools for doing it well. It doesn't eliminate discomfort, but it makes people more open to learning, listening, and growing. It supports better communication, decision-making, and collaboration.

Gratitude helps leaders give direct feedback without creating defensiveness. It allows teams to process failure and keep trying. It fosters a sense of trust and safety, enabling new ideas to flourish. And it prevents fear from taking over in the face of uncertainty.

Once, while teaching a leadership workshop, a participant asked why their manager, despite using all the recommended communication techniques, still had bad communication. Our answer, we figured out together: "He leads from fear and negativity." That moment stuck with me. Techniques can only go so far. When gratitude is present, communication becomes clearer, more authentic, and more effective. It builds trust. That's the ripple effect of gratitude.

What this means for you as a leader is to not just apply techniques; infuse them with authentic gratitude if you want the message to land.

Final Thought - Garbage In, Garbage Out (GIGO)
Very little from my Computer Science degree has stayed with me; Fortran and Pascal are long gone from my memory. One principle remains crystal clear, and it applies directly to AI: GIGO. Garbage In, Garbage Out. AI is only as good as what we feed it and how we use it. Data is at the heart of everything related to AI, says Justin Evans, author of *The Little Book of Data*. However, data is information, not action. It's leaders who put it into action. If you want

accuracy and ethical actions, you cannot feed AI misleading, dishonest, or incomplete information.

Think back to the 2008 financial crisis: lenders distorted the financial realities of individuals and companies, approving mortgages that should never have been issued. Standards were ignored, data were falsified, and billions were lost because decisions were based on garbage inputs. Another, more subtle example is how averages can hide the truth. In 2016, the average caseload for the Department of Children and Families in Massachusetts appeared reasonable on paper; however, a closer look revealed that some caseworkers had one case, while others had over 30, and the impact was life-altering. Reporting and making decisions based on averages alone masked the reality of the situation and led to dangerous misjudgments.

The lesson is simple: Embrace gratitude. Think carefully. Developers, test thoroughly and demand integrity in your data. Users, question, and validate the ethics embedded in every system you adopt. Leaders, ensure ethical practices and enforce guardrails.

The world will keep changing. AI will keep advancing. Crises will rise and fall. Leaders who anchor themselves in gratitude and stay connected to their people, their values, and their humanity will shape a future built on trust and meaning. Gratitude won't stop change, but it will help you move with it, lead through it, and come out stronger on the other side.

The future of leadership isn't just about learning new tools; it's about staying human. Gratitude is what makes that possible.

The Human Advantage Takeaways
- Change is inevitable. Gratitude makes it more manageable.
- The COVID-19 pandemic highlighted the power of gratitude to steady and strengthen us during times of crisis.
- AI is a transformative force that requires human-centered leadership.
- Gratitude improves communication, trust, feedback, and decision-making.
- Leaders who practice gratitude model openness, courage, and clarity.

Reflection Questions
1. How do you typically respond to change? What would it look like to respond with more gratitude?

2. What role will AI play in your workplace and life over the next 1–5 years?

3. How can you use gratitude to strengthen your leadership during uncertain times?

Chapter 6
Leadership, Vision, and Models

In the long history of humankind (and animal kind, too), those who learned to collaborate and improvise most effectively have prevailed.
~ Charles Darwin

In leadership literature, the words *gratitude*, *appreciation*, *recognition*, *positivity*, and *praise* are appearing more frequently. Seven years ago, only a handful of leadership books discussed gratitude. It was rarely indexed and often treated as an afterthought, sometimes replaced with recognition or appreciation. Today, a few modern leadership models are grounded in gratitude, signaling its rising importance. Gratitude isn't just a nice-to-have; it's a key skill for leaders.

Vision Paired with Gratitude

Leaders have followers. Leaders have a vision, whether they are aware of it or not. The followers follow the vision of the leader, whether they are aware of it or not. The more followers, the more likely the vision will come to fruition. Gratitude helps leaders clarify and stay present to the vision that pulls them forward. The vision inspires and influences followers. Gratitude and the vision together create the clarity and energy that people want to follow.

Simon Sinek's popular TED talk first labeled the "Why" as the purpose, cause, or belief that drives you. Why is a leadership model. By weaving gratitude into your leadership practice, you don't just talk about why you feel it, live it, and invite others to do the same. That alignment transforms routine tasks into meaningful contributions and turns organizations into movements. Operating from our Why is inspiring and makes us more human, exactly what is needed in the age of AI.

Why is the reason your organization exists. When the Why is clear, everything becomes easier and more inspiring, such as decision-making.

Workplaces use many terms for this future state of making your Why happen: vision, mission, direction, intention, strategy, program, initiative, scope, outcome. Regardless of the word, the leader's role is to take people from where they are now to someplace new. That requires change.

Gratitude makes change possible in a positive and sustainable way. It builds resilience, curiosity, and trust, qualities that help people move through discomfort. Together, the qualities create sustainable momentum for more positive results.

What this means for you as a leader is that when you lead with vision and gratitude, people don't just follow; they believe.

Examples of Simplified 'Why' Statements

Leader	Future Direction / Why
Mahatma Gandhi	Movement: Non-violent resistance
Nelson Mandela	Vision: Reconciliation through forgiveness
Mother Teresa	Mission: Serve the sick and poor
Ken Olson	Intention: Engineering excellence
Oprah Winfrey	Direction: Empowerment through media
Taylor Swift	Mission: Empowering women through music
Tom Brady	Goal: Excellence in football
Caitlin Clark	Goal: A positive sports role model
Project Manager	Scope: Deliver on time, on budget
VP of Product	Initiative: All products are AI-enabled
Director	Outcome: Reduce complaints
Star Dargin	Vision: All leaders embrace and strengthen their gratitude

THE GRATITUDE GAP

As someone who's worked with leaders in multiple industries, I've seen firsthand how leadership models rise and fall, but the ones that endure are grounded in human connection. Gratitude is increasingly at the center of that.

In a world shaped by data (both good, bad, and neutral), human-centric algorithms have become a strategic necessity for leaders.

There are hundreds of leadership models. A quick Amazon search turns up over 70,000 books. Depending on the source, there are between 15 and nearly 100 prominent models. According to the HR Trend Institute, almost 100 leadership models are currently in use. Leadership models are constantly evolving, often overlapping or customized to suit an organization.

When I asked both ChatGPT and Google Gemini which leadership models and mindsets are most effective in the age of AI, they pointed to transformational and change leadership, along with strategic vision, emotional intelligence, and data-informed decision-making. Yet, neither mentioned gratitude.

Curiously, when I asked how important gratitude was to leadership, both AI platforms gave glowing endorsements:

"Gratitude is a powerful tool for leaders to create a positive, productive, and engaging work environment." – Google Gemini, February 24, 2025

"Gratitude is crucial for leaders because it fosters a positive work environment, strengthens relationships, and enhances overall team performance." – ChatGPT, February 24, 2025

Leadership Model: How Leaders Work

Most effective leadership models, especially those relevant to AI and change, are implicitly human-centric and gratitude-aligned. Here are a few leadership models I have direct experience with and how gratitude fits into each:

Servant Leadership: Focusing on serving the needs of others first is the essence of servant leadership. The term was first introduced by Robert K. Greenleaf in his 1970 essay *The Servant as Leader*, written decades before the rise of AI, when "others" clearly referred to humans. In the essay, Greenleaf stated:

"The difference manifests itself in the care taken by the servant-first to make sure that other people's highest priority needs are being served. The best test, and difficult to administer, is: Do those served grow as persons? Do they, while being served, become healthier, wiser, freer, more autonomous, more likely themselves to become servants? And, what is the effect on the least privileged in society? Will they benefit or at least not be further deprived?"

The servant model prioritizes serving the people over AI, profit, and even the leader. Gratitude and servant leadership are deeply interconnected models. They both foster positive cultures and build trusting and caring relationships among people. Servant leaders help their followers improve through appreciation, feedback, open communication, understanding, and positive relationships. They engage with them in meaningful ways. The downside of servant leadership that I have seen is that it becomes a crutch for some leaders to never learn how to assert their own voice, and they become unseen. In that silence, gratitude shifts from a source of strength to a habit of self-erasure and coping.

Emotional Intelligence (EI): This model has existed since the 1960s and has since evolved. Daniel Goleman brought the term to a broader business audience. He researched and wrote a best-selling book that shows direct ties between leadership success and what he labels as the key skills for EI: self-awareness, self-regulation, motivation, empathy, and social skills. Other variations of EI, such as EI assessments, training, and books, exist. Gratitude and EI are intertwined. Each EI skill builds on and promotes the growth of the other. It's a chicken-and-egg relationship. Self-awareness enables you to identify and acknowledge positive emotions, fostering a deeper understanding of yourself. This, in turn, leads to more effective responses and choices (self-regulation), motivating you to pursue what you enjoy. Strengthening my gratitude has been the single most critical skill in being able to emotionally respond in the moment rather than ruminating on it minutes and weeks later. EI is typically the weaker skill for the very logical thinking leader in my coaching practice. Gratitude builds stronger empathy and social skills. When you have strong relationships, gratitude is present.

Radical Candor: Coined by Kim Scott in her book *Radical Candor: Be a Kick-Ass Boss Without Losing Your Humanity*, this model is about caring deeply while challenging directly. It's about holding opposites, being kind and firm, open and honest. This directly contrasts with a lesson I learned early on from my mother: "If you can't say something nice, don't say anything at all." That well-meaning guidance became a limiting belief. It took me years to realize that kindness isn't the same as niceness. Nice avoids discomfort; kind embraces it for the sake of growth.

Radical Candor demands that we show up with care, even when it's hard, and that's exactly what gratitude trains us to do. It's easier to give and get feedback when it's grounded in appreciation and recognition.

Gratitude makes feedback more human and easier to receive.

Liminal Leadership: A newer model that focuses on leading through transitions. It overlaps with Transformational Leadership and William Bridges' classic Change Theory. These models focus on helping people navigate uncertainty and the "in-between" space of change between old and new. Leaders who are thinkers, who often resist uncertainty, do well when they acknowledge that there is and we are in a liminal in-between place in time. Gratitude grounds leaders in that ambiguous space, offering steadiness when clarity is not immediate. Gratitude builds hope and connection in liminal moments.

The Gap and the Gain: Dan Sullivan and Dr. Benjamin Hardy's model encourages high achievers to focus on what they've gained, not what they lack. It's all about appreciation. They also connect appreciation to meaning. They write: "The things we value or appreciate the most also have the greatest meaning." Gratitude transforms the gap into a gain by shifting attention from what is lacking to what is meaningful, reminding leaders that progress is measured in appreciation, not perfection. Changing one's thinking changes the mindset belief of 'never enough' or 'not good enough', which in turn improves performance.

Wait There's More

In addition to the leadership models mentioned above, my previous book, *Leading with Gratitude*, and the many leadership books I read and reviewed over 32 months, all include gratitude, either explicitly or implicitly, in their frameworks.

Gratitude Builds Collaboration and Engagement

Leaders are not leaders without followers. Regardless of the leader or the models used, gratitude is not just personal; it's civic. Positive psychology identifies gratitude as a "vital civic virtue." It energizes people to act morally, helps build meaningful relationships, and prevents destructive behavior. Robert Emmons, one of the top researchers on gratitude, writes that it allows us to become "participants in our lives instead of spectators."

Gratitude creates engaged workplaces. It builds the trust and psychological safety needed for true collaboration.

AI vs. Humanity

Leadership and how you lead becomes even more important in the world of prevalent AI. AI is increasingly human-like in how it interacts with us. Some AI platforms adapt to our personalities. They trigger feel-good chemicals when they affirm our ideas or actions. That feedback loop can become addictive. Just like with video games, people with strong gratitude are better at maintaining perspective and not using AI as a crutch for human relationships and connections.

Final Thoughts
Change is constant. Gratitude is foundational. Vision is what pulls us forward.

Leaders can choose how they move through change.

Gratitude won't create a vision. But it will make it easier to believe in one and make your vision happen.

Gratitude will make you the type of leader people want to follow and partner with to achieve the vision.

Leadership, Vision, and Models Takeaways

- Gratitude is increasingly present in modern leadership models.
- Gratitude alone is not leadership; it must be paired with vision.
- Gratitude fits into all leadership models and makes them stronger.
- Gratitude fosters engagement, trust, and change-readiness.
- Leaders who pair gratitude with a clear Why are more effective.

Reflection Questions

1. What leadership skills do you use now, and how well do they handle change and uncertainty? And how do they pair with gratitude?

2. Which leadership models resonate with you or your organization?

3. What is your Why/Purpose/Vision? For you as a leader and your workplace? What future are you trying to create?

PART III
The Paradox of Gratitude
Navigating what's simple and what's hard.

Truth #3: Gratitude Is Easy and Challenging

This part explores the paradox of gratitude, simple to understand, easy to do once, yet challenging to maintain. Offering insights on measuring, mapping, facing, and solving the very real challenges that leaders encounter.

Gratitude is when memory is stored in the heart and not in the mind.
~ Lionel Hampton, Jazz Legend

We are Wise

Chapter 7
Measure, Track, Grow

Measure what is measurable, and make measurable what is not so.
~ Galileo Galilei, astronomer, physicist, and engineer

Gratitude Truth #3: Gratitude has (often invisible) challenges. And those challenges create the gap between knowing and doing.

You already know gratitude make everything better (Truth #1) and that it's a skill you can strengthen (Truth #2). But building and sustaining gratitude is harder than it sounds. Gratitude can fade under stress, get overlooked in busyness, or feel impossible in the middle of a challenging moment. That's the Gratitude Gap.

Think of it like physical fitness: strength, flexibility, balance, and cardio all matter. You need all four to stay healthy, and each takes effort to maintain. Gratitude works the same way.

Many people don't know what their gratitude challenges are. Others don't feel they have time. Some may not know how to apply gratitude in high-stress situations. Gratitude Truth #3 highlights that the obstacles are unique and real. But they are not insurmountable.

Build Your Gratitude Baseline

Gratitude may be invisible, but it can be measured. To find your personal gratitude baseline, you can start by rating yourself on a scale of 1 to 10 in these three areas:

1. **Consistency - Sustaining Gratitude**: What percentage of your average day are you grateful? A score of 10 means you think about and approach everything with gratitude, even the most difficult, frustrating, or mundane.

2. **Depth - Feeling Gratitude Fully**: How deeply do you feel gratitude? A 10 means full-body, heart-and-soul gratitude, the kind that shifts your entire being and how you move through the world. I first felt this kind of depth after the birth of my children. Someone described it this way to me: "It's when every cell in your body lights up."

3. **Shifting - Returning to Gratitude**: How fast can you get back to gratitude after stress or difficulty? A 10 means you can shift to gratitude almost instantly, even while still in pain or discomfort. Wendy's story of shifting to gratitude after just

receiving a diagnosis of cancer is an example. She is still in touch with the reality of her diagnosis and is gratefully handling it. She has a strong gratitude baseline. A low number for shifting might mean it takes time to return to gratitude. For me, it took me a few decades before I could say I appreciated a sleazy manager I once had; gratitude wasn't immediate. Eventually, though, I realized through gratitude that I learned from the experience. That, too, is a sign of shifting.

Rate yourself 1-10 in each area to discover your baseline. Use this to measure your progress over time. Reassess yourself every few months, or at least annually.

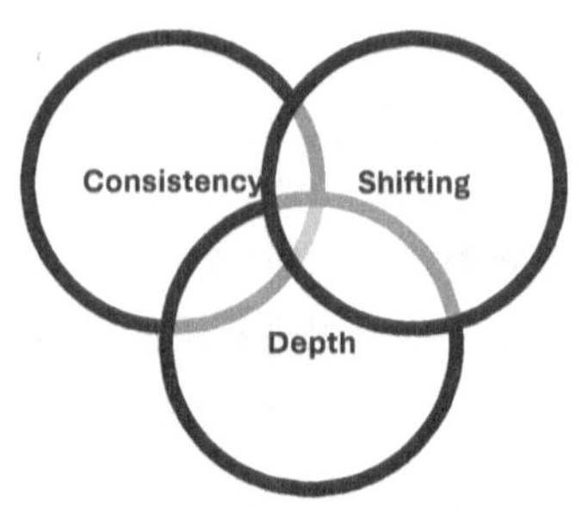

Already scoring high in one or more areas? Great. But take a closer look. Baselines are only useful if they reflect reality. You can't improve what you can't measure, and with something as invisible as gratitude, that takes honesty. Someone once explained it to me this way: if you're moving too quickly to gratitude, you are probably skipping over something difficult, you're not building strength, you're dodging the workout. That's a form of toxic positivity, using gratitude to bypass reality. Be especially mindful if your score feels too easy to achieve. Are you truly feeling it, or just performing it?

Tailoring Measurement: One Size Doesn't Fit All

The baseline assessment was created from years of reading gratitude research and practical experience. It only includes the three areas: consistency, depth, and shifting, to make it easy and simple. However, because everyone's gratitude challenges are different, you might want to expand your baseline measurement to include:

- Physical environments (home, office, nature)
- Community (friends, family, neighbors)
- Behavior patterns (saying thank you, writing notes)

These additional data points help create a richer, more personal picture. Just be consistent when measuring.

In the workplace, gratitude can be tracked in simple and effective ways:

- Recognition systems
- Appreciation check-ins
- Inclusion in 360-degree feedback

One team I know starts every team meeting by counting appreciations. Another asks: "Did you feel appreciated this week?" These practices turn gratitude into something visible and cultural.

What this means for you as a leader is that when you measure gratitude, yours and your team's, it allows you to spot strengths, identify blind spots, and lead more intentionally.

That's why your baseline is not static; it gets tested in real life. One moment, your gratitude may be flowing; the next, it's blocked by stress, deadlines, or exhaustion. Measuring your gratitude helps you stay aware and responsive rather than reactive. It keeps you anchored. As Peter, a CTO and self-described "Chief Thank You Officer," once said, "The biggest challenge to practicing gratitude is … life."

What this means for you as a leader is that, by tracking gratitude over time, you build emotional resilience and help others do the same.

Gratitude in Diverse Workplaces

The more diverse your workplace, the greater the variation in gratitude. Differences show up in how people express, expect, and receive appreciation. These variations arise from personality, culture, age, gender, industry, religion, and even introversion vs. extroversion.

For example, introverts may dislike public recognition. It could feel awkward or even disrespectful. A private thank-you note would be more meaningful. On the flip side, some extroverts are disappointed when appreciation isn't loud or public.

In some cultures, saying "thank you" is expected. In others, it's rare or even odd. In parts of Southeast Asia or West Africa, thanking someone aloud may seem strange or unnecessary.

Just because you express gratitude doesn't mean it was received as intended. Gratitude is woven into the social fabric of cultures. And it can backfire if it doesn't resonate.

Gratitude Strength Shows Up in Moments

How long does it take to build a strong gratitude practice? The answer ranges from 20 seconds to 20 years.

That's why measuring your baseline helps. It gives you something to measure and track.

The benefits of gratitude often sneak up on you. It took me over a decade to realize how much I had changed. One moment that revealed my strong gratitude baseline was when I broke my ankle. Even while sitting in searing pain with my leg elevated, I found myself laughing. Maybe it was the shock, but I was also flooded with appreciation: for not getting hit by a car, for my cellphone, for my husband who came to get me, for the warmth of our house in winter, and for access to medical care. I was grateful and in pain simultaneously.

Another story I often share is about a friend who used to experience intense anxiety before medical procedures. After years of practicing gratitude, she described being wheeled into surgery and noticing that she was calm, something she called a breakthrough. That moment confirmed her inner strength. One more friend used to get enraged when cut off in traffic. One day, after being cut off, he kept driving, unfazed. It wasn't until his wife pointed it out that he realized how much he'd changed. He credits his shift to consistent gratitude and meditation practice.

Years ago, I would have forced a smile and said something nice, just like my mother taught me. Now, I'm grateful I can say something real, kind, respectful, and honest even when things are hard.

In addition to measurement, your visible success will be in your reactions, your habits, your stories, and how others talk about you.

Gratitude Is Free (but Takes Time)

Gratitude is an unlimited resource, as abundant as air. It costs nothing to use. Learning how to overcome challenges is both easy and hard. For those concerned about cost, the good news is that the only cost is time. Of course, you can pay for apps, beautiful journals, courses, or for me to teach leaders gratitude, but it's not required.

"If they only knew the benefits of gratitude, they'd practice it all the time," one grateful leader told me.

I wish every leader could experience the benefits for themselves and for the people around them.

So, start now. Measure your gratitude. Build your baseline. Practice regularly. Uncertainty is a guarantee for leaders. You never know when you'll need the strength that gratitude provides.

Measure, Track, Grow Takeaways

- Gratitude is free, but building a strong practice takes intention and time.
- Gratitude is defined and expressed differently across individuals and cultures.
- A gratitude baseline includes depth, consistency, and shifting back to gratitude.
- A gratitude baseline is one way to measure gratitude strength, and it's also in behavior changes and stories.
- You can personalize your baseline with physical, community, and behavioral elements.
- Workplace gratitude can be measured in practices, behaviors, and outcomes.
- Gratitude builds strength for life's inevitable challenges.
- Gratitude Truth #3 acknowledges that there are unique and real challenges.

Reflection Questions

1. Create your gratitude baseline. How would you rate yourself (1–10) on:
    - o   a. Gratitude consistency
    - o   b. Depth of feeling
    - o   c. Ability to shift back to gratitude after difficulty

2. Answer the interview questions in the Leadership Gratitude Question Chapter at the end of this book about your relationship to gratitude.

3. Interview a leader, especially one very different from you, using the Leadership Gratitude questions. Compare your answers and look for new insights.

Chapter 8
Common Gratitude Challenges

Every challenge, every adversity, contains within it the seeds of opportunity and growth.
~ Roy Bennett, Author

Leaders often excel at spotting other people's gratitude blind spots and miss their own. As Brené Brown, a researcher, storyteller, and Texan, reminds us, you need people in your life who "speak truth to your bullshit." That's why having trusted colleagues or a confidential feedback review is essential. These truth-telling colleagues care enough to deliver honesty with respect and sensitivity even when it hurts because they know that honest insight, though uncomfortable, accelerates growth.

In this chapter, we'll explore the most common blind spots, unconscious habits, and real-world misfires that keep even well-intentioned leaders from expressing authentic gratitude and how to overcome them.

Over the years, I've identified roughly fifty common gratitude challenges. I formally interviewed thirty people, recording each conversation with the same set of questions, and surveyed many more. My interviewees spanned industries, roles, and seniority levels. You'll find the interview questions in Appendix A and a summary of challenges in the final chapters. Some challenges overlap or lie beneath conscious awareness. Hundreds of solutions exist, some tried and true, others surprising, and many solutions apply across multiple challenges.

Big Challenges: "Enough" and "Discernment"

Two subtle but powerful hurdles stand out. First, the "grateful enough" myth: the idea that once you've said 'thanks' or feel appreciative, you're done. Second, the challenge of discernment, holding seemingly opposite emotions, like fear and gratitude, at the same time. When leaders learn to spot and work through these, they unlock deeper authenticity, resilience, and trust.

Challenge: "I'm Grateful Enough"

One senior manager believed she was grateful enough, until anxiety paralyzed her before her company's first in-person post-COVID national leadership meeting. Colleagues held fiercely opposing views on politics and pandemic policy, and she feared a "shipwreck meeting." Working together, we listed what she genuinely appreciated: the leaders' passion, the company's mission, and paired each item with her anxieties. By acknowledging both gratitude and fear, she was able to take actions that worked and allowed the meeting to happen and be successful. She started by establishing clear ground rules and flexible seating options. The meeting became a resounding success because she held both anxiety and appreciation in the same frame. It wasn't until she consciously paired gratitude with her anxiety that she could lead effectively.

Challenge: Discernment, Holding Opposites

Dr. Scroggs, a social psychologist whom I interviewed about gratitude, taught me about discernment by telling the story of her husband totaling their only car. She first reacted by sulking and ruminating on the huge inconvenience of broken plans, repair costs, and lost convenience, and felt no gratitude for the accident. But within hours, she intentionally decided to be grateful. She appreciated her legs and public transportation. She laughed as she told me she was glad she no longer had to remember where she parked her car on trips into the city. In that moment, she wasn't grateful *for* the accident, but she could appreciate what it revealed.

That's discernment: not pretending the hardship didn't happen but expanding your awareness to include what else might be true that you can appreciate.

Language Shapes Leadership

Some challenges are straightforward to identify and stubborn to change; word usage is an example. Our habitual language shapes neural pathways and frames our reality.

From "Have To" to "Get To": After attending one of my gratitude talks, an attendee was so excited to hear someone else talk about this that he tracked me down to share how a colleague's feedback had changed his life. He realized his habit of saying and thinking, "I have to," kept him stuck. He replaced his thinking about it from every "I have to" with "I get to," transforming thoughts of "I have to go to a meeting" into "I get to go to a meeting" and turning obligation into appreciation. His mindset and, within weeks, his life shifted profoundly.

From "Problem" to "Opportunity": I noticed that a tech executive I coached labeled every challenge as "the problem." While logical for someone in tech, this mindset painted people and situations in a negative light by labeling them as problems. When he consciously reframed his language for people, calling each issue an "opportunity" instead, he unlocked greater empathy and creative thinking. For example, when a direct report relied too much on his feedback, instead of considering that a problem, he called it an opportunity. As an opportunity, he then learned how to coach the person to find more of their answers.

Three months later, both his professional performance and personal satisfaction had improved dramatically.

Changing a single word or phrase changes your mindset, and your mindset shapes everything else you do.

How to Give and Receive
Leaders often stumble over the mechanics of gratitude. One-size-fits-all doesn't work: people differ by personality, generation, and culture. Understanding these differences lets you customize your appreciation, so it lands authentically.
Real-world misfires I've witnessed often come from well-intentioned leaders whose gratitude simply didn't land. Common unintentional mistakes include:

- Using offensive or outdated phrases
- Comparing someone to a public figure they admire but the other person doesn't
- Calling the entire team "amazing," even when the performance level of individuals varies
- Offering generic or inauthentic praise rather than naming real, not-so-good impact
- Ignoring real challenges and giving only surface-level thanks

Some managers believe employees shouldn't expect appreciation for doing their paid job; others feel awkward acknowledging routine effort. I coach leaders to look for genuine contributions, not just outcomes, and to practice SMART gratitude and remembering to appreciate both the person and the task.

Here's a framework to make your gratitude S.M.A.R.T.:

S	Specific. Describe exactly what they did that you appreciate.
M	Measurable. Note the impact or difference they made.
A	Authentic. Be genuine and honest in your appreciation.
R	Realistic. Make it practical and believable.
T	Time-Bound. Say when the behavior to appreciate occurred.

You don't need to include every element every time, but the more you do, the more meaningful your appreciation becomes. For example:

"When you submitted the quarterly report two days ahead of schedule, it helped our team stay on track. I appreciate your efficiency and foresight."

Compared to a generic "Great job!", SMART gratitude shows real attention to detail and makes your appreciation memorable.

When you tune into individual preferences and cultural cues, your gratitude sticks.

What this means for you as a leader is that your gratitude only has impact if it's received. When you tailor it to fit the person, you deepen connection, trust, and engagement.

Common Gratitude Challenges Takeaways

- The two most impactful blind spots are the belief of being "grateful enough" and the skill of discernment. Address these two first, and many other challenges fade.
- Word-usage habits, whether thinking or saying them like "have to" versus "get to," or "problem" versus "opportunity," are simple; they are not easy to change, yet when you do, they create powerful transformations.
- Everyone's gratitude challenge is unique; some challenges are invisible.
- Honest feedback from a coach or trusted colleague is critical for surfacing gratitude challenging blind spots.

Reflection Questions

1. Which gratitude challenge discussed in this chapter resonates most with you, and how has it shown up in your leadership?

2. Identify one habitual phrase you use (e.g., "I have to," "the problem"). How could you reframe it to foster gratitude?

3. Who could serve as a truth-telling colleague for you, someone who will speak authentic feedback about your gratitude blind spots, and how will you engage with them?

Chapter 9
The Dark Side of Gratitude

When someone shows you who they are, believe them the first time.
~ Maya Angelou, Poet, Author, Activist

Gratitude abuse has many forms, from scripted flattery by salespeople to inauthentic announcements by CEOs, orchestrated disinformation on social media, and charismatic cult leaders demanding repetitive expressions of thanks. It's unethical and abusive when gratitude becomes a tool for manipulation. Abusive gratitude removes choice and exploits our impulse to respond positively, hijacking our brain's natural feel-good chemicals, from dopamine surges to oxytocin-driven trust, to influence behavior.

When Influence Becomes Manipulation
Influence is neutral: it invites someone to choose. Manipulation predetermines an outcome at the expense of another's freedom. There is a fine line between influencing and manipulating. The science

of influence, which is part of many sales and marketing playbooks, doesn't come with a moral compass. Without a moral compass or knowing that moral boundaries are different for everyone, the lines between influencing and manipulating are crossed. Here are some examples:

- **Scripted flattery** in sales settings, "You look absolutely stunning today," aims to close a deal, not build genuine rapport.
- **Corporate pronouncements** of faux appreciation serve image rather than connection.
- **Disinformation campaigns** on social media cloak persuasion as "heartfelt thanks."
- **Cult leaders** demand repetitive gratitude as loyalty tests, suppressing dissent and choice.

Manipulation of gratitude is a form of gratitude abuse. It's forcing the feel-good chemicals on someone for an advantage. I find it fascinating to watch gratitude abusers in real life and in fiction.

Gratitude abusers can be charming and someone you want to hang out with, trust, and confide in. Consider cinematic con artists Leonardo DiCaprio in *Catch Me If You Can*, Bradley Cooper in *American Hustle*, and Paul Newman and Robert Redford in *The Sting*. More recently, Netflix's *Inventing Anna* dramatizes Anna Delvey's charm.

In real life, Charles Ponzi was active in the early 1900s, convincing roughly 40,000 investors to hand over an estimated $15 million with promises of fivefold returns. More recently, Bernie Madoff orchestrated his version of the Ponzi scheme through the stock market, raising billions from clients. His fraud unraveled in December 2008 when more investors requested withdrawals than he had assets to cover.

The U.S. Justice Department then created the Madoff Victim Fund, distributing $3.2 billion to nearly 37,000 victims, recovering only about 80 percent of total losses. Both Charles and Bernie made people feel good; they were reported to be charismatic, personable, and highly respected.

Even one of my gratitude heroes, Elie Wiesel, Nobel Laureate and Holocaust survivor, devoted his life to finding and teaching gratitude amid suffering. His resilience is so powerfully evident in his book *Night*. He wrote that while in a concentration camp, he was grateful for food. Yet that same openness left him and his Foundation vulnerable to Bernie Madoff's betrayal, which cost them $15 million. Reflecting on the betrayal, Wiesel said, "We thought he was God; we trusted everything in his hands." His story is a powerful reminder: gratitude and trust are strengths, but they must be paired with critical awareness, or they risk being exploited.

Delvey, Ponzi, and Madoff were smart, and they carefully crafted their personalities. They are con artists; in workplace terminology, this is sometimes called a "corporate sociopath" or "snakes in suits".

Today, AI can amplify manipulative tactics and extend their reach. Bad actors, scammers, and even well-meaning users now have tools to fake data, images, voices, and emotional tone with realism. These individuals use data-driven personalization to craft emotionally resonant messages and deep-fake voices or images that trigger subconscious trust.

This raises a new challenge: How do we discern real gratitude from rehearsed or programmed responses? As more AIs become capable of sounding grateful, *how will you train yourself and your team to recognize the difference and behave appropriately?*

Staying present, emotionally attuned, and grounded in your values becomes even more essential. This is not just about tech literacy; it's about *gratitude literacy.*

Gratitude Abuse of Ourselves

We can also deceive ourselves by forcing or faking gratitude to avoid discomfort. In the short term, we feel better; in the long term, we build pressure cookers of unaddressed stress, eroding trust, and our overall well-being. Faking gratitude in relationships sows distrust; faking it at work damages authenticity, which erodes trust.

When Zeal Turns Counterproductive

Sometimes, well-intentioned enthusiasm for gratitude can become rigid or overbearing or outright threatening. For instance, some self-described gratitude "warriors" push compliance with their approach without recognizing that people approach gratitude in different ways, at different paces, and from different lived experiences. What begins as encouragement can feel more like pressure. Authentic gratitude meets people where they are; extremist zeal shuts them out.

Here are some examples of how I've seen overzealous gratitude backfire:

- Requiring or expecting people to "be grateful or else" without honoring their discomfort or struggle. A person threatened to hit someone unless the other person was grateful.
- Using one-size-fits-all, my-way-or-the-highway advice (aka, mansplaining) without regard to individual challenges. A person preached to me that journaling was the only way to cultivate gratitude.
- Forcing constant positivity or ignoring reality. A workplace was collapsing (and eventually went out of business), yet the leaders never

acknowledged or dealt with the industry reality that was constantly put in front of them.

- Overlooking that each person's journey with gratitude and their comfort zone is unique. Personally, I've been accused of not appreciating something when I truly did. As a quieter, sometimes introverted person, I was grateful, but I didn't know how to speak up authentically.

The truth is: forced gratitude creates resistance and overlooks reality. Authentic gratitude invites people in. It meets them where they are, not where we think they should be.

As with all leadership practices, gratitude works best when it's intentional and there is awareness, rather than by rote.

Overcoming Dark Gratitude

Part of the solution is to cultivate strong gratitude so that you are mindful and present. Staying open and aware in the moment is crucial. Staying gratitude-savvy is your best defense.

Consider using this checklist of gratitude and ethics to determine if your gratitude is authentic or if someone expressing gratitude to you is being authentic.

Ethical Checklist for Giving or Receiving Gratitude

Expectation:

> When you give: Am I expecting something in return?

> When you receive: Are they expecting something in return?

Spontaneity:

> When you give: Is my praise scripted or genuinely spontaneous?

> When you receive: Is their praise scripted or genuinely spontaneous?

Consent:

> When you give: Does the recipient feel free to accept or decline?

> When you receive: Do I feel free to accept or decline?

Power Dynamics:

> When you give: Am I leveraging my position to compel gratitude?

> When you receive: Are they leveraging their position to compel gratitude?

Clarity of Intent:

> When you give: Is my aim to serve others or advance my agenda?

>> When you receive: Is their aim to serve others or advance their agenda?

You can use this checklist in real time before meetings, emails, or in appreciation moments.

Manipulators, con artists and scammers expect something in return. They shove gratitude down our throats. **Why this matters to leaders** is that authentic gratitude builds trust and gets results. Inauthentic gratitude doesn't and it can be hard to identify. The stronger your gratitude, the more likely you are to detect inauthentic gratitude.

Authentic gratitude meets people where they are and expects nothing in return.

The Dark Side of Gratitude Takeaways

- Influence leaves choice intact; manipulation takes choice away. Strong self-awareness in gratitude protects you from manipulation.
- Con artists have been creating personalities that flood our feel-good chemicals so that we can be influenced and taken advantage of more easily. AI will make it easier to be conned.
- Real gratitude carries no strings; it's given freely, with nothing expected in return.

Reflection Questions

1. Where have you experienced gratitude used manipulatively, at work or in the media?

2. How might you be unconsciously faking gratitude to avoid discomfort?

3. What guidelines can you set up to ensure your expressions of gratitude remain authentic?

PART IV
Gratitude Breakthroughs
Closing the gap

Challenges and Solutions

In these chapters, you'll confront the messier side of gratitude, from toxic positivity to translation errors, while uncovering practical techniques and mindset shifts that transform obstacles into opportunities for growth.

Acknowledging the good that you already have in your life is the foundation for all abundance.
~ Eckhart Tolle, spiritual teacher and author

We are all in the same boat.

Chapter 10
Definition Challenges

Every time you communicate, you have an opportunity to introduce something that positively influences others.
~ Sam Horn, Writer, Coach, and Speaker

Ask twenty people how they define gratitude, and you'll get twenty answers. Ask them to dig deeper, and based on their definitions, they will share the many different ways to communicate and show gratitude, some welcome, some offensive, and some natural. Some ways we show gratitude contradict each other, and some are complicated "mental gymnastics." This lack of definition consensus can stall leaders because of the lack of communication.

Gratitude can trip us up just as easily as it lifts us. Definitions can become hurdles that stall even the most committed gratitude leaders. Part of what makes gratitude challenging is that the meaning shifts from person to person.

That's why I'm offering a working definition:

Gratitude is a foundational skill, a way of being and doing that is rooted in appreciation. It is practiced through intentional habits, tools, and behaviors that strengthen mental, emotional, and physical well-being.

For leaders, this means gratitude is not abstract. It is practiced. Successful leaders build gratitude, use its tools, practice it regularly, and resolve gratitude challenges.

This definition gives us common ground to move forward beyond confusion, culture, or personal preference. From here, we can explore how gratitude works in leadership and how it shows up in daily habits, systems, and choices.

I once spoke with a leader who wanted to launch a peer-recognition program. He struggled with questions: Should awards be public or private? How will high performers react when less experienced colleagues are honored? What criteria feels fair to everyone? As his uncertainty grew, the project stalled and so did the chance to build a culture of appreciation. Clear definitions and criteria could have kept it moving.

Introducing the "Gratitude Wall"

A Gratitude Wall shows up when authentic thankfulness flows easily in one area (home, organization, work, team) but stops short in other areas. Sometimes it's a silent culture cue; sometimes it's tied to identity or belief. You can feel expressive at home yet reserved at work or vice versa. The key is noticing the gap, then asking: What's the definition here?

One leader realized she praised her team openly and regularly but forgot to show warmth at home. Another leader was the opposite; he was extremely grateful at home and not at work. He left gratitude at home because his definition of gratitude was tied to his deep religious life. Once each of these people became aware of how they defined gratitude and the wall it had created, it sparked change in both of them.

Before reading on, jot down your definition and beliefs about gratitude.

Even dictionaries can't agree: some focus on feelings, others on acknowledgement or benefits received. I surveyed four major dictionaries when writing this, and all defined gratitude slightly differently.

Contrasting Experts' Definitions

Dr. Robert Emmons, leading gratitude researcher, calls it a relationship-strengthening emotion in two steps: affirming the presence of good and recognizing its source outside ourselves. "Gratitude requires us to see how we've been supported and affirmed by other people," he writes.

Dr Brené Brown describes gratitude as an emotion reflecting deep appreciation for what we value and what connects us. She notes that joy, contentment, and gratitude share a core ingredient: appreciation.

Barbara L. Fredrickson, a professor and researcher on positivity, says of gratitude in her book, *Positivity*, "True gratitude is heartfelt and unscripted." It's not tit for tat or reciprocity, you scratch my back and I'll scratch yours. She goes on to identify the gratitude challenge, which she calls gratitude's evil twin: indebtedness. True gratitude doesn't create a debt.

Cicero called gratitude a **virtue** and said, "Gratitude is not only the greatest of virtues but the parent of all others."

In **Positive Psychology,** gratitude is a **character strength**. It is one of the twenty-four-character strengths that shape you. You can take a free self-reported assessment test to see how your gratitude rates as a character strength.

Gratitude is my top character strength; however, I know it is not how others necessarily see me and would describe me. That is why I am continually working on my gratitude challenges. I continue to strengthen my top character strength of gratitude to be stronger and reflect externally.

Defining Workplace Gratitude

Respect, that's gratitude. This is how Steve Kadish defines gratitude in the workplace. Kadish, a Democrat, was the first chief of staff for Massachusetts Governor Charlie Baker, a Republican. Their problem-solving approach was non-partisan, service-oriented, and results-driven. Throughout his administration, Baker was repeatedly recognized as one of the most popular Governors in the nation. They co-authored a book describing the Results Framework titled *Results: Getting Beyond Politics to Get Important Work Done.*

Here's how Steve defines gratitude in the workplace: *It's respect. It's the completion of respect regarding one another, listening before speaking, acknowledging messages and being timely with responses, and being aware of how you ask questions and talk with your colleagues, whether they are higher-ups, peers, individuals reporting to you, or the consultants and others that you may work with. It's one of the things that I think is vital in getting things done. It creates environments where people are comfortable dealing with the uncomfortable. It's hard to do in a hierarchy because you have a person three or four levels down in a meeting, and there's a CEO or the head of their unit. How does that question need to be asked and answered in a way that's respectful, that elicits honest dialogue, that moves the meeting from a reporting session to learning and problem-solving? That's gratitude.*

A Spectrum of Definitions

Definitions vary: some see gratitude as a feeling, while others see it as a habit or a value. From my interviews, I received over twenty definitions of workplace gratitude; the respondents' replies fell along a spectrum into these categories:

- **Emotion:** Appreciation, Thankfulness, Sincerity
- **Habit:** Practice, Muscle, Approach
- **Principle:** Value, Character Trait, Religion
- **Metric:** Recognition, Feedback, Measurement

Gratitude Attributes

In addition to the various definitions, gratitude has these attributes: it is on a spectrum, is interpreted differently, is inclusive, and is about contrast.

Gratitude is on a spectrum. It isn't an on/off switch. You might feel every cell in your body swell with thankfulness one moment and anger, fear, or frustration the next. *Example:* When a teammate stays late to help you meet a critical deadline, you feel profound gratitude; minutes later, that gratitude may ebb when they deliver blunt feedback on your work.

Gratitude is filtered through interpretation. We all bring a different lens to gratitude: personality, culture, mood, and past experiences. *Example:* A public shout-out thrills one person and mortifies another.

Gratitude is inclusive. True gratitude holds opposites together. It's an "and" that welcomes both joy and challenge, appreciation and critique. *Example:* You're grateful for a promotion AND aware of the increased responsibilities it brings, embracing both excitement and the pressure to perform.

Gratitude through contrast. We often recognize gratitude most clearly when we've lived its opposite. Hardship, loss, or scarcity deepen our appreciation for health, stability, and abundance. *Example:* After recovering from a serious illness, each healthy day feels like a gift, made richer by the memory of sickness.

What Is Not Gratitude

Not everything labeled as "gratitude" truly is. It's easy to confuse gratitude with other behaviors – such as politeness or positivity that sound similar but lack emotional substance. Consider these common pitfalls:

- **Obligatory politeness:** A perfunctory "thank you" said by rote, like saying "thanks" for an automatic email notification, lacks genuine appreciation.

- **Reciprocity:** When you do something nice solely to receive something in return, that's a transaction, not gratitude. Expecting favors undermines authentic thankfulness.
- **Blind optimism:** Believing everything will work out without acknowledging challenges misses complexity. It's like assuming guaranteed job security or convincing yourself you'll win gold in gymnastics at age 50. Optimism without grounded awareness isn't gratitude.

Stories of Misplaced Gratitude

A friend told me about a colleague who runs a non-profit foundation. At every board meeting, she showered leaders with praise, but it felt insincere; her compliments were generic and expected. Her team learned to tune out her gratitude entirely. **Takeaway:** Sincerity beats volume; empty praise quickly loses its impact.

In the old South, people say "bless your heart," which can mean genuine sympathy … or quietly signal condescension. The exact words can convey warmth or criticism. Gratitude language can mask judgment. **Takeaway:** Context shapes meaning; clear intent prevents misunderstandings.

During a recognition event at a global tech firm, leaders applauded in unison for each awardee, but the applause was timed to music cues. Employees later said it felt more like a rehearsed performance than a true celebration. **Takeaway:** Authentic gestures create genuine connections, not staged rituals.

These examples highlight that gratitude isn't just words or rituals; it's sincerity, context, and connection.

In many workplaces, gratitude is often confused with other positive words and is often overshadowed by terms like appreciation, recognition, or praise. Gratitude is more than appreciation, recognition, and praise. It's the foundation that they sit on. Sometimes cultures overuse gratitude language until it feels hollow.

Gratitude is also lumped in with many other positive states, feelings, and words. Gratitude's closely related cousins are optimism, joy, serenity, hope, amusement, inspiration, awe, and love. "Happiness is murky and overused," says Barbara Fredrickson in her book *Positivity*. Happiness suffers the same challenge as gratitude, in that it is broad and ill-defined.

Gratitude as a Foundation

Positivity and happiness are similar entry points as gratitude to improving our lives by keeping those feel-good body chemicals around longer. Gratitude is the foundation that positivity and happiness sit upon. Consider these three extreme example situations and their relationship to gratitude, positivity, and happiness.

- **Death of a loved one:** You can grieve deeply and still be grateful for their life. Positivity and happiness won't be present.
- **An unplanned crisis:** Gratitude helps you manage and move forward, and positivity may surface, even if happiness does not.
- **A joyous event:** Gratitude, positivity, and happiness are present.

Situation	Gratitude	Positivity	Happiness
Death	Y	X	X
Unplanned Crisis	Y	Y/N	X
Joyous Event	Y	Y	Y

Gratitude is the steady ground, the foundation, that carries us through every circumstance.

The stronger the foundation of gratitude, the longer positivity and happiness can last. Define gratitude clearly for yourself, your team, and your workplace, and you create a shared foundation. Gratitude then moves beyond feeling; it becomes an actionable and powerful force for leadership.

Definition Challenges Takeaways

- Definitions of gratitude vary widely and change over time. The definitions share common threads: appreciation, connection, and recognition.
- Experts agree that gratitude strengthens social contribution and connection.
- Gratitude has four key attributes to consider: spectrum, interpretation, inclusivity, and comparison.
- Not everything that looks or sounds like gratitude is gratitude.
- Here's a useful way to define gratitude for leaders. Gratitude is a foundation. It is a skill, a set of tools, habits, and behaviors that strengthen physical, social, and mental health.

Reflection Questions

1. How do you define gratitude? Write a clear, concise statement of what it means to you.

2. Which attribute of gratitude (spectrum, interpretation, inclusivity, comparison) resonates most? Why?

3. Where do we hold back on gratitude? Where does our gratitude wall exist? What's one step you can take to tear it down?

Chapter 11
Stress Buster Techniques

*We must see all scars as beauty. Okay? This will be
our secret. Because, take it from me, a scar does not
form on the dying. A scar means, "I survived."*
~ Chris Cleave, *author*

Stress-inducing events, such as spilling coffee or
being yelled at, will always happen. The amount of
stress for each situation varies for individuals.

Then there are the life-altering, stress-inducing
events like divorce, death, and disasters. They can be
unconscious stress-inducing events, like noise or a
smell associated with a prior bad experience.
Smelling smoke may evoke a pleasant memory of fun
times around campfires. For others, the smell of
smoke may cause stress because it unconsciously
signals the presence of a devastating fire or of being
in a war zone.

Stress can make us feel scared, frustrated, angry, anxious, or nervous, and is a natural, healthy, and normal reaction to any potentially
dangerous situation.

Unconscious Triggers

A senior leader I coached recognized he was stressed whenever he had to talk to one of his competent peers in person. He was a very grateful person, yet he had an immediate dislike of this person and held onto it for years. He was stressed around her and never felt thankful for her, and he didn't know why. When we dug into it, he discovered that her perfume reminded him of his ex-wife, with whom he didn't have a good relationship. Identifying the unconscious stressor allowed him to transform his relationship with his peer into a positive and professional one.

Gratitude doesn't remove stress, but it softens its grip and restores perspective. The more grateful we are, the less stress we experience. Why? Because gratitude improves our awareness, we are open to overriding the body's natural stress response. We get to choose our response. The challenge is that what may cause stress is different for everyone. There are general and obvious stressors, like emergencies, but each leader is unique in what causes them stress and how they respond. Staying constantly stressed is not healthy. The more quickly we can identify and handle stressors appropriately, the healthier it is for us and those around us. Gratitude helps us unlock and become consciously aware of our stress signals and helps us choose to respond differently.

Twenty Seconds or Twenty Years to Transform
Building on gratitude as a foundation, the following stories show how the first moments of awareness can catalyze change, whether it takes seconds or even years.

I froze the first time someone yelled at me in a business meeting. I was almost thirty, proposing a technology they didn't support, and my body shut down, caught in a biological survival response. The VP yelling at me was many organizational levels above me, and for years, that moment haunted me.

Over time, I learned self-awareness and stress relief techniques, but the real turning point came when I added gratitude. Gratitude gave me the pause I needed to process, to choose my response, and eventually to see him with more understanding. Ironically, that same VP became my manager two years later, and I gained far more from him than I ever expected. Looking back, I'm grateful for that difficult moment, because it forced me to grow into someone who no longer freezes when being yelled at and can respond appropriately.

I know gratitude helped me in ways I didn't even realize. Decades after starting a regular gratitude practice, an account representative called to let me know I was being removed from leading my favorite workshop at a well-known scientific research company. I was so angry during the phone call. She couldn't see it, but my hands turned into fists, and my whole body tightened up. All I wanted to do was scream at her about how unfair it was. In my head, my response was defensive. I wanted to yell at her that it didn't make sense because I was receiving the highest level of feedback possible in reviews. Instead of yelling like I wanted to, I remained quiet. *In the twenty seconds of quiet, I paused, took a deep breath, and asked myself what I was grateful for in this situation.* I was grateful for the opportunity and camaraderie and for working with these brilliant scientists.

Pausing and asking the question changed my thoughts and shifted me to gratitude. When I felt grateful, I said in a calm voice, "That's not what I want. Is there anything that we can do so I can still work with them?" That conversation led to some interesting insights, and I delivered another workshop to them. I later learned she wanted me to leave so she could put her friend in the position. If I had not turned to gratitude, I would have lost the workshop, not learned some valuable lessons, and probably lost the whole account.

I still get stressed when someone yells at me. I recognize now that being stressed is a normal and healthy response. However, the difference is that I am aware of being stressed and have learned how to handle it. I choose my response. Unconsciously, I now pause, take a deep breath, focus on the situation and what's needed, and shift to gratitude so I can handle the situation within seconds.

When I first learned to shift to gratitude, it wasn't unconscious. I had internal conversations with myself. The conversations went something like this: I'd tell myself what was going on; for example, they were yelling, I was angry, I sounded defensive, or I was stressed or frozen. I had to label what was happening to figure out the next steps. Then, once I've shifted to gratitude, I choose my response. Do I need to protect myself, walk away, speak up, yell back, show caring and compassion, or listen?

As I drafted this chapter, I faced a triple-threat home emergency: a gas leak, a septic overflow, and a power outage before a snowstorm, all within 12 hours of each other, while I was alone in an isolated area. Instead of panicking, I felt focused and resourceful, grateful for the swift help and safe resolutions.

Nothing blew up, nobody was hurt, and I walked away with lessons and procedures to manage and prevent future crises.

Even now, I don't always feel grateful in the moment, and that's okay. I wasn't initially grateful when my triple-threat home emergency happened, or back when someone yelled at me in a meeting. It took *decades* to find gratitude for that difficult workplace experience, but only *seconds* during the triple threat.

The difference was awareness and practice. In the home emergency, my first thoughts were crystal clear: identify the biggest threat to handle, take action, and stay safe. Gratitude kept me calm and focused. What once took me years to process now takes moments. That's the power of gratitude, it transforms reactions into responses and stress into steady, purposeful action. The regrets and ruminations don't stay with me; the situations are handled, and the stress dissipates faster.

Out of these hard lessons, I developed two simple practices that anyone can learn and use:
- **Three-Step Shift to Gratitude**: A step-by-step guide to gratitude in any moment, especially when stressed.
- **Back-Pocket Question or Statement**: Personalized prompts that redirect your mindset toward gratitude when stress strikes.

These originated as I analyzed my stress response to being yelled at and losing an important client.

Three-Step Shift to Gratitude
The goal of the Three-Step Shift is to be able to move to authentic gratitude so that you can approach any situation, no matter the difficulty, with gratitude. Shifting to gratitude activates the feel-good chemicals in your body, which opens up awareness and allows you to see more of reality to make better choices. If you make gratitude a habit, eventually it will happen unconsciously. The three-step framework below is how I teach it and use it myself. You may need to modify it to work for you.

1. Notice — Awareness that you are not grateful. Something has negatively triggered you. Notice what you are saying, doing, thinking, and feeling. This acknowledges what is happening within you and the situation. This can be triggered by something external, such as a person or situation, or internal, such as a feeling or thought. It can also be triggered unconsciously. The more you can uncover the trigger, the easier it is to insert a new positive behavior.

2. Shift — Pause and reflect on your current reality. Here are some ways to shift to gratitude in the moment:

- Take a few deep breaths.

- Offer a quick prayer and ask for guidance.
- Get curious about the situation.
- Observe yourself in a detached way (thoughts, body, emotions).
- Use your Back-Pocket Question or Statement silently or out loud.

3. Act – Once you feel gratitude, choose your response. Options include:

- Do nothing
- Take direct action
- Change your tone, words, or gestures
- Prioritize and plan
- Validate the reality with others
- Escalate or seek assistance
- Lead, coach, or facilitate collaboration

Back-Pocket Question or Statement Technique

Back-pocket statements or questions help you shift to a state of gratitude and handle the unexpected.

Prepare them ahead of time for triggers you've identified. Then, when stress arises, pull out your back-pocket prompt to stay grounded.

Here's some examples to ask yourself in the moment:

- "What am I grateful for about this situation?"
- "Will this matter in five years?"
- "What's the worst that can happen?"

- "What do I know for sure?"
- "What's the big picture here?"
- "What do I want and how can I help?"

When you are grateful, respond in a calm and measured way. Then move to action, which could be: do nothing, walk away, listen, respond, decide, or act. If you decide to stay in the discussion in real time, other examples of back-pocket responses are:

General acknowledgment (not agreement):
- "Thank you."
- "Interesting."
- "I hear you."
- "Let me make sure I understand you. Did you say ABC?"

Wanting to know more:
- "Please say more."
- "Can we go back and explore more about…?"
- "Help me understand why…"
- "Humor me, why might this be a bad idea?"
- "Is there another perspective I'm missing?"

Deflect or Delay:
- "What does [other person] think?"
- "Can I get back to you?"
- "There's something more here I can't put my finger on."

If it's a virtual meeting, consider putting the back-pocket statements or questions on a sticky note for your eyes only as a reminder.

I worked with a group of senior leaders in the software and AI technology space. They are passionate and genuinely care about their work. They are brilliant and have strong opinions. They shared with me that they might sometimes label or even call someone (out loud) stupid, dig their heels in on a point, or stop listening. When I taught them the back-pocket questions, two weeks later, during an accountability check-in, the results were excellent. The answers and results they obtained were different, enabling them and others to see a more comprehensive and holistic view of changing reality. They did admit it was not easy, and they had to remind themselves of what they had put in their back pocket.

What this means for you as a leader is that when you are grateful, you can transform chaos into calm leadership. Gratitude keeps you in the moment, taking action to solve problems now rather than later.

Stress Buster Techniques Takeaways
- Stress itself is not bad; it's a signal to pay attention. Constant stress is unhealthy, but gratitude offers a healthy counterbalance.
- Stress varies from everyday hassles to traumatic events; your triggers are unique.
- Two core techniques, Three-Step Shift and Back-Pocket Prompts, help you move into gratitude and manage stress.
- Stress is inevitable. Gratitude doesn't erase it, but it gives you the power to choose your response.

Reflection Questions
1. Practice the Three-Step Shift on a minor stressor (e.g., traffic). Experiment with different gratitude shifts: pause, breathe, ask, or state. What do you notice?

2. Create and test multiple Back-Pocket Questions or Statements that work for you. What do your back-pocket questions or statements say about your beliefs?

3. List triggers that pull you away from gratitude. Reflect on any patterns and consider strategies to anticipate them.

Chapter 12
Ted Leads with Gratitude

The truth is, everything will be okay as soon as you are okay with everything. And that's the only time everything will be okay.
~ Michael A. Singer, American spiritual teacher, author, and former software entrepreneur

Imagine a mission-driven workplace where everyone looks forward to meetings that flow purposefully: attendees arrive on time, prepared with valuable insights, and listen without interruption. In under an hour, a complex problem is solved through respectful debate, no backchanneling or gossip, only trust and collaboration. Participants leave early, energized, and clear on next steps. This culture of appreciation is real: in my many informal surveys, only one in ten professionals participated in such a meeting. I'm grateful to have experienced this type of workplace; most only imagine it.

How would a grateful leader create a workplace like that? Learn and teach gratitude. Ted Lasso is fictional and entertaining, yet he is representative of the grateful leaders I interviewed and have worked with. In real life, challenges don't resolve neatly in ten or twelve episodes.

Gratitude Expert Ted

At the heart of Ted's approach is a conscious practice of gratitude that shapes every action and interaction.

Ted Lasso is a sitcom about a syrupy-sweet midwestern football coach transplanted to lead a premier United Kingdom football team (soccer for those in the United States). It is one of my all-time favorite shows, which I've watched multiple times and talk about in my leadership workshops. It has been nominated for sixty-one Primetime Emmys and numerous other awards. According to entertainment critic Richard Roeper, the pop culture references in Ted Lasso "fly faster and more frequently than a string of expletives from Roy Kent when he's in a particularly verbose mood."

Ted created a supportive and positive workplace that led to wild success. Success for the fictional story was winning games and learning, growing, becoming strong, enabling trust, building lasting relationships, and having fun. All were led by Ted using his positive leadership style. Gratitude is a fundamental skill and theme throughout each episode.

The show is engaging and deeply human. It has the right mix of story, action, and character development. From his recruitment as a naïve U.S. football coach in season one, episode one, Ted was able to create a successful, world-class U.K. football team in three seasons based on the principles of positive leadership.

This scene from season two visibly upset me when I watched it:

Nate is yelling at Ted, yet it is Nate who has screwed up big time! Ted transforms Nate's career from clubhouse attendant to assistant coach. However, Nate's appreciation transforms into resentment in the second season. When Ted discovers Nate's unhappiness, he invites him to talk, whereas most leaders would have ignored him or not known something was wrong with their employees. Ted is proactive.

In a private conversation, Nate told Ted, "Everybody loves the great Ted Lasso. Well, I think you're a f*cking joke... You don't belong here." [Gulp.] Then Nate turns on Ted. Despite the sting of betrayal, Ted responds not with anger but with listening and curiosity. Most leaders would get defensive; Ted turns it into an opportunity to understand. That's gratitude in action, transforming adversity into growth.

Have you ever faced someone yelling at you at work who you think you are supporting? It's devastating. What would you do? For many people, it would cause them to fight back, get defensive, run away, move into the dark side, and not be grateful. Ted stayed positive and calm; he listened. Ted genuinely wanted to learn what was bothering Nate and fix the issue.

Eventually, almost everybody loves Ted: the players, the fans, the media, and the barflies. Even though he is unique, he is authentically positive and himself. He is jarring and awkward until you get to know him. Ted creates a positive culture that brings out the best in people and teams. The players strive to perform better by constantly learning, showing appreciation, believing in themselves and the team, and showing empathy. Importantly, Ted handles the hard stuff in a positive way.

Ted faces the gratitude challenge of toxic positivity. When Ted doesn't address the reality and anxiety of his failing marriage, it causes him to have an anxiety attack. He eventually gets professional counseling help, which transforms and deepens his leadership and self-awareness. In turn, it also improves his relationships and the team's performance.

Ted's Techniques
Ask "What can I learn?"
Instead of opening with blame, Ted asks, "What do I have to learn here?" This shift assumes shared responsibility, fosters open dialogue, and turns challenges into growth opportunities.

Stay calm and curious
When faced with criticism or conflict, like Nate's harsh words, Ted centers himself, listens without judgment, and resists defensiveness, modeling composure under pressure.

Be curious, not judgmental
Quoting Walt Whitman, Ted reminds his team to "be curious, not judgmental," creating psychological safety by seeking understanding before evaluation. There is an excellent "dart" scene that highlights this behavior. Ted wins a significant bet because people aren't curious and tend to underestimate him.

Appreciate the person, not the task
By saying "I appreciate you," Ted honors individuals for who they are, not just their soccer skills. What they do is acknowledge their intrinsic worth and the effort they put in.

Embed simple gratitude rituals
Ted makes gratitude tangible and shares it. He encourages teams to pause, reflect, and start fresh

together. Ted creates a sign with one word, "Believe," that becomes a physical symbol of their hope, optimism, and gratitude. The sign takes on a role of its own and serves as a reminder.

Gratitude to Resolve Challenges

It would not have been an interesting show if Ted had always been positive and happy, without resolving challenges and achieving results. The show is inspiring and focuses on Ted's growth, as he uses positivity to help those around him resolve issues in each episode.

Sports is an excellent analogy to workplaces. They strive to win and have time-bound (seasons) goals. Sports have many ups and downs; each game is a new opportunity to perform. Sport practices are similar to gratitude practices. You do it to get stronger and better and hope that when it's game time (workplace challenges), you win.

Ted Lasso finds the positive in everything. Leaders with gratitude actively search for the positive. They see the harsh reality and the positive, but don't stay stuck. At the end of season one, the team experiences a devastating loss and is demoted to a lower division.

They are crushed, and the mood is somber in the locker room. For some, there is nothing to be grateful for. Despite this, Ted gives them hope; he finds something for them to be grateful for and hang on to.

Here's his locker room speech, which allows the negative and the positive to exist simultaneously:
TED: I want you to be grateful that you're going through this sad moment with all these other folks. Because I promise you there is something worse out there than being low, and that is being alone and being sad. Ain't nobody in this room alone.

The goldfish metaphor is another metaphor Ted uses to keep it real and move away from getting stuck in the negative.

"Do you know what the happiest animal on earth is? A goldfish," Ted tells Sam, one of the high-performing team members, after he underperforms. "Why a goldfish? Because they have a ten-second memory and can quickly start fresh and stronger by putting failure in the past."

The goldfish metaphor appears multiple times throughout the show's three seasons. In this dialogue, Ted acknowledges the complex reality of the situation, provides space for sadness, anger, or failure, and then moves on. He leads by teaching and building on the concept of goldfish.

TED: What do you think we should all do once we get done being sad and/or angry about this situation?

SAM, AFC Richmond Player: I think we should all be goldfish.

TED: I agree. Let's be sad now, let's be sad together, and then we can be a gosh darn goldfish.

Ted is a composite of the grateful leaders I know, know of, and have interviewed. These leaders faced personal health crises, prison, near suicide, betrayals, and other tragedies that they came through. Gratitude was one of the main reasons that they attributed to moving forward. All the examples are now available for you to use and adapt.

Ted is authentically Ted. He's quirky, awkward, and inspiring, and he doesn't hide it; he walks his talk. His behavior aligns with who he is, and he strives to be a positive leader. Like the way Ted Lasso seeks to be authentic, gratitude will help you discover your inner and authentic self and share it with the world.

What matters to leaders is that even though Ted is fictional, I've seen similar situations firsthand in workplaces. Try making a game of it, watch it, and keep a checklist of what you've seen and had to deal with in your workplace. The fictional aspect and humor make it relatable and an excellent source for leaders and teams to play and explore how gratitude can be strengthened in the workplace.

Ted Leads with Gratitude Takeaways

Ted Lasso is fictional, but the gratitude-based behaviors he models are real and transferable.

Here are some core practices you can adapt to your own leadership:

- Remain proactive and positive with challenges and difficult conversations. Ask, "What did I do wrong here?" instead of, "What's wrong? What's bothering you?"
- Stay curious under pressure. Ask, "What can I learn here?" instead of leaping to blame or judgment.
- Appreciate the person, not the task. Try, "I appreciate you," instead of "I appreciate what you did" to affirm intrinsic value, not just output.
- Always look for the positives in the negative. Everything is a lesson.
- Acknowledge both the positive and the negative. Acknowledge setbacks honestly, then shift like goldfish toward what's next.
- Use simple gratitude rituals. Symbols such as Ted's "Believe" sign remind teams to reset, stay hopeful, and move forward together.

Ted's greatest strength isn't perfection; it's authenticity. He leads as himself. The challenge for you is the same: adapt these practices in ways that align with your genuine self. Gratitude works when it's real.

Ted reminds us: gratitude isn't about being perfect or positive all the time. It's about being real, being curious, and leading in a way that brings out the best in others.

Reflection Questions

1. What leaders (fictional or real) do you know who create positive environments?

2. How do they create positive workplaces?

3. Watch a video clip of a Ted Lasso scene (there are some in the Reference section) and note what Ted does to create a positive environment.

Chapter 13
I'm Fine, Toxic Positivity

Maybe you have to know the darkness before you can appreciate the light. The eye is always caught by light, but shadows have more to say.
~ Gregory Maguire, author

Toxic positivity is the belief that you must stay positive about everything, even when it doesn't make sense. It's gratitude given too soon, happy words plastered over a wound, like telling someone who just lost a client, "Smile. It's not that bad."

David Kessler, grief expert and author of six books on loss, defines toxic positivity as "positivity given in the wrong way, in the wrong dose, at the wrong time." Left unchecked, it becomes a habitual bypass: a way to ignore, repress, or deny difficult realities, leaving us stuck without the full view of reality that we need to heal and grow personally.

In workplaces, this inability to see the whole picture hinders our ability to improve performance and results. Toxic positivity ranks among the most significant challenges because it can infiltrate and undermine an entire workplace culture.

When "I'm Fine" Isn't Fine
Our initial reactions in moments of pain, regardless of their size, can set the stage for toxic positivity or genuine empathy. Imagine you've had a bad day, the coffee machine doesn't work, or you lost a big client.

You vent to three people: your friend, your coach, and your partner.

Your friend: "Everything will be alright."
You reply, "Yes, of course. I'm fine," yet your chest still tightens.

Your coach: "There's a lesson in this."
You nod, then seethe, wondering if they truly hear you.

Your partner: "Let it go."
You want comfort, not a check-the-box pep talk.

Each response, though well-intended, can slip into toxic positivity when it cuts off honest feelings. If you move on too soon, smile through the ache, you are practicing toxic positivity.

Reframing for Authentic Gratitude

Instead, imagine responses that acknowledge your pain first:

- Your friend paused and said, "I hear you, it's rough. I'm grateful you shared this with me."
- Your coach asked, "You're upset. What do you need right now before we look for lessons?"
- Your partner might say, "I see you're hurting. How can I support you?"

Authentic gratitude holds space for both darkness and light. It acknowledges sorrow, then invites hope, on your terms.

Spotting Toxic Positivity

Over the years, I've collected the following phrases frequently used in toxic positivity situations. On their own, they seem harmless, but when offered too soon or without acknowledging pain, they shut down honest feelings, stall growth, and in the workplace limit how problems are solved and the results achieved.

This categorized view highlights how similar phrases serve different (and sometimes conflicting) functions; context, delivery, and timing determine whether they offer comfort or cut off genuine connection.

Statement that May or May Not be Toxic Positivity

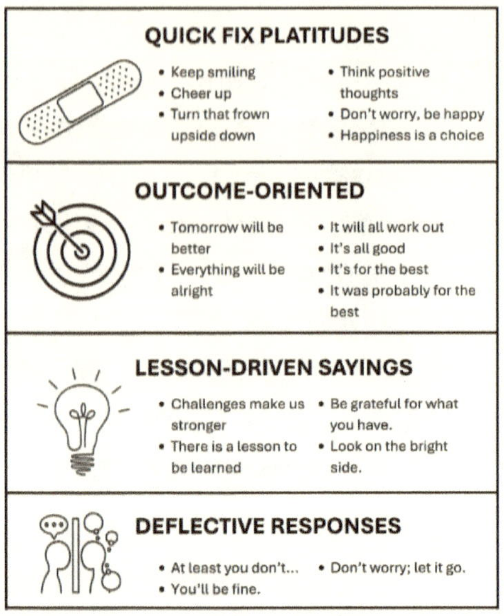

The Cost of Denial

Persistent toxic positivity erodes trust and honest connection. It keeps the focus of the conversation on the surface, rather than on the reality of difficulties or challenges. Decisions and actions are limited. It becomes a vicious cycle when problems are ignored, and we see a pattern of ongoing comments, such as "It will get better," "It was only one time," and "They don't mind."

Being overly positive can cover up unspoken truths. Lynne was a single woman who had a surface-level friendly relationship with her next-door neighbor for years. Lynne was warm and outgoing, a beautiful, happy person, but whenever she tried to move past small talk with him, she was met with polished platitudes of toxic positivity.

It wasn't until Lynne casually mentioned her 4 a.m. exercise class that the facade broke. The neighbor realized he'd misjudged her completely: he'd assumed she was coming home late from nights out, when in fact she was rising before dawn to work out.

As they laughed and cleared up the misunderstanding, their friendship deepened in a way no amount of surface-level platitudes could achieve.

Judgment clouds relationships, and trust suffers when truth is sidestepped. You don't know another person's story until you are willing to go beyond the surface.

Even heroes of gratitude can easily slip into toxic positivity. Ted Lasso's panic attack, brought on by ignoring the painful reality of his marriage, reminds us: real gratitude lives in reality, not denial.

From Toxic to True
Learn to identify when others push you to positivity before you are ready to shift to gratitude. Here are some situations that have been detected by leaders

who kept logs of when they stepped over something and became positive to avoid a difficult situation:

- Conflict avoidance. They switched topics to fun topics.
- Not knowing an answer. They made a joke instead.
- Gossiping. They gushed positively about the person, even if it wasn't true.

These are all real situations from my coaching clients, who, once they recognized their avoidance of the problem, learned how to shift to gratitude and handle the difficult situation.

When you catch yourself or others racing to positivity, pause. A simple breath or "I need a moment" buys time. Notice avoidance patterns: changing topics, joking away tension, or plastering on a smile.

Choices in the moment
- **Name it:** "I'm really struggling right now."
- **Hold the Negative:** Sit with discomfort for a moment of honesty.
- **Shift it:** When you're ready, find a genuine gratitude spark, a lesson learned, or a small comfort. Learn the three-step shift to gratitude. Toxic positivity prevents deeper conversations and the inclusion of the whole truth in decision-making and action-taking. It keeps things stuck, never advancing, and always staying within a

limited view of reality. Toxic positivity keeps leaders and workplaces stuck or worse, sliding backward.

Creating Non-Toxic Workplaces

As a leader, you can model and create workplaces that are not toxic. Start by verbalizing and discussing failures, frustrations, and anxieties. Don't dwell, just acknowledge. Here are some specific actions to try:

- Don't mandate gratitude or happiness; pair gratitude with reality: look for what we're grateful for in every failure.
- Model failure. Tell real stories of your own mistakes. Bill Treasurer, author and consultant, says: "Too many leaders make themselves the hero of the story... It's far better to tell a story where you got it wrong. It makes people trust you more."
- Don't ignore mistakes, reframe them as lessons. There is a gift, a lesson in every mistake, if you look hard enough.
- Model how to apologize and acknowledge your errors.

Authentic gratitude isn't about plastering on a smile; it's about seeing the whole truth, light and shadow together. Gratitude allows for a holistic, neutral, and non-judgmental approach. When you name it, hold it, and then shift, gratitude becomes a tool for growth instead of denial. Not creating or continuing workplaces of toxic positivity matters to leaders because it dismisses real struggles. Toxic positivity bypasses truth instead of building resilience. You acknowledge both hardships and gratitude simultaneously, which creates trust, psychological safety, and hope.

I'm Fine Toxic Positivity Takeaways

- Toxic positivity limits our choices and responses; it is not gratitude.
- Toxic positivity shows up when positive statements are used in the wrong way, in the wrong dose, at the wrong time.
- Toxic positivity uses gratitude to avoid something.
- Individuals and workplaces can suffer when truths get bypassed.
- Toxic positivity is nuanced and situational; it can be given or received, conscious or unconscious.
- Learn to identify toxic positivity patterns.
- To shift from toxic positivity to true gratitude:
    - o 1. Name it. "I'm really struggling right now."
    - o 2. Hold the Negative. Accept the discomfort without rushing past it.
    - o 3. Shift to Gratitude. When ready, find a genuine thing you're grateful for.

Reflection Questions

1. Recall a time you rushed to positivity. How did it feel then? What was overlooked? How might you respond now?

2. Which toxic-positivity phrase do you hear most often, and in what context?

3. Who in your life models authentic gratitude? What do they say, or do, and how do you know it's authentic?

Chapter 14
Confronting Negativity

Be prepared to appreciate what you meet.
~ Frank Herbert, author

Roxanne, a talented and hardworking project manager, quit after seven years of flawless service, covering holidays and crises without ever hearing a genuine "Thank you." Her manager was shocked; Roxanne had been one of the company's best employees. Appreciation never voiced is appreciation never felt. She isn't alone. In my previous book, I share how Sue, a medical lab technician with the highest accuracy rating, left her job for the same reason. Both stories highlight a painful truth: failing to express gratitude drives away great talent.

Staying grateful in a negative workplace or around negative people without sounding like a goody-two-shoes or Pollyanna is energy-draining and challenging. It's contagious. It can bring us down and make it difficult to get work done efficiently. Good ideas might be scrapped before they see the light of day. Motivation and engagement are low, and procrastination is high with negativity. The challenge is not to let the downers bring you down.

There are numerous discouraging statistics regarding negative managers and workplaces. The impact is that people do not feel appreciated or engaged, and eventually, they leave their jobs, resulting in the business suffering. According to various studies, some of the top reasons people leave are that they are not respected or appreciated by their direct manager.

Expressing gratitude is a simple and easy thing; it would have made all the difference and kept both Roxanne and Sue as employees.

Negativity exhausts us, spiking stress hormones and depleting feel-good chemicals, undermining our resilience. It's not healthy; it creates unnecessary stress. The stronger our gratitude, the less likely we are to be sucked into someone else's negativity.

Walking away from a person or situation is sometimes the best course of action; however, as a leader, it's not always possible. Sometimes, managing a negative person or interacting with them is the job. Sometimes, it's your job as a leader to change the workplace so that it's not negative.

No matter how hard we try, sometimes our gratitude is not contagious to everyone. For whatever reason, some people remain negative. Everything they say is a "No," "We can't," "Here's what's wrong," or silent dissent.

Changing someone else is almost impossible. We can only change ourselves. As a leader, you can be a role model by modeling grateful behaviors. However, direct attempts to change a person who is unwilling to change will most likely be met with resistance.

As a leadership coach, my role is to help individuals make positive changes. I start by getting clarity on their coaching goals. The most successful people I have coached are open and ready for change. They are positive and appreciative to have a partner in their forward movement.

I learned the hard way not to take on every person who wants to hire me as a leadership coach. There are some people I will not work with: those who are unwilling to change and those who are negative and reluctant to learn or take responsibility for how their behaviors impact others. When someone interviews me to be their coach, I am also evaluating their willingness and motivation to change. I don't want to waste my time or theirs and their money. However, leaders in the workplace are not so fortunate and often don't have a choice in who they work with. A strong foundation of gratitude counters this.

The solution to negativity is strengthening your gratitude so you are immune to negativity's contagiousness. Strong gratitude will naturally repel negativity and enable you to develop a more effective response to negative people.

Changing a workplace culture is challenging. In a successful workplace, individuals work together toward a common goal. Leaders help shape and direct the culture of individuals toward that goal, requiring change.

Daniel Coyle, who wrote *Culture Code*, emphasizes that the main attribute of a supportive culture is a safe environment in which members feel valued, belonging, and appreciated. This type of culture connects individuals, making them feel safe and fostering strong chemistry that enables them to work as a cohesive unit. Cultures that experience highs and lows together, stick together, and acknowledge their shared humanity, even in difficult times, remain cohesive.

Changing a workplace to a positive one starts with the leaders. Leaders create culture. If leaders are skilled at showing gratitude, the culture will naturally reflect it. The higher up in an organization, the more influence a leader has, the larger their impact.

As a leader, cultural change is a journey of behaviors and processes to support gratitude. It takes time and starts with the foundation of gratitude.

Negative Bias

I was surprised that many truly grateful leaders I interviewed did not come from a background that included gratitude. At some point in their lives, they had to learn gratitude. For one leader, it was simply asking the question each night at dinner, "What are you grateful for?" instead of complaining about the day.

For another, it was learning to notice. The first time she shifted to gratitude was as a young adult, when she saw a flower growing in a crack on a city sidewalk.

For many, it was experiencing life-changing, horrific events that made them understand how grateful they were for life.

A gratitude approach doesn't come naturally to many people and may not be part of the culture in which you were raised. Many people begin their lives by focusing on the negative and must learn to consciously cultivate gratitude.

You can blame our DNA for always starting with a negative approach. Negativity bias is a gratitude challenge that keeps us on the dark side of gratitude.

Negativity bias occurs when we focus on negative information more than positive information. It was a necessary survival skill for our ancestors. It allowed them to see everything as a threat so they, and we, could survive.

Negativity bias once kept our ancestors alive: better to assume a rustle in the bushes was a tiger than risk being wrong. But our brains haven't caught up; today, the same survival wiring kicks in during bad meetings or tough feedback situations, rarely life-threatening. Gratitude helps recalibrate that bias, so we see the whole picture instead of defaulting to the dark side.

But negativity doesn't just live in our DNA; it shows up in people and workplaces, too. As a leadership coach, I've seen both the impact of negative bias and the challenge of working with people who resist change.

I've delivered hundreds of confidential 360-degree feedback sessions with leaders. These sessions involve me sharing the patterns and themes that I've identified through collecting feedback from their bosses, peers, employees, and sometimes customers and personal connections. Most of the 360-degree feedback I've received about the leader is stellar and glowing. However, a small percentage (1-5%) of negative feedback ruins their day, week, or career when they become overly focused on or obsessed with it. Instead of the positive, they focus on the negative. That is the negative bias at work, focusing on the gap instead of the gain. In contrast, grateful leaders appreciate all feedback, reflect on it, view it as a valuable lesson, and use it as a source of information, sometimes as an opportunity to change or grow.

Negative bias causes people to focus more on the negative, even when receiving a compliment. Receiving a simple compliment like, "What a great job you did", with a negative bias, they would not believe the compliment and instead focus immediately and reply with all the things that went wrong and could have been done better. Alternatively, they may not respond to the compliment or believe the person, which can erode trust.

If you know someone with a negative bias, you can adjust how you show appreciation. You can also try being specific or acknowledging a negative. For example, instead of "You did a great job," try SMART gratitude. An example of SMART gratitude is "The task ABC was overall excellent, there is still work to be done, and you have overcome these two specific (list them) challenges today."

Culture of No: My Router Ordeal

Recently, I had a real-world test of gratitude under fire, in a customer service situation. I had 24 hours before I needed my Zoom video on my laptop to work, and I had no Wi-Fi. After hours of online chat (on my phone) and phone calls with service reps, it was determined that the equipment was at fault, and I needed a new modem/router.

Customer service offered me two choices: drive over an hour to the nearest service center or wait for a delivery window that would miss my deadline. They repeatedly assured me the store would honor a swap. Armed with screenshots of their promises, I ventured out.

The service center, in a rundown strip mall, was tiny and uninviting. Inside were two idle reps. Every request met with a curt "no":

- No sharing of the recording of my chat, and granting me a new router
- No replacing the equipment or getting new equipment
- No access to the account, it was my son's
- No testing of the old equipment

Their dismissive tone sparked my frustration and anger, but I kept shifting back to a state of gratitude. I reminded myself this was their procedure, not a personal attack. With persistence (and a call to corporate), I finally walked out with a working router, after an hour-long ordeal that should have only taken five minutes. Gratitude didn't erase the hassle, but it kept me from escalating into a fight that would have gotten me nowhere.

People Who Test Our Gratitude

Sometimes, slimy, repulsive, or dishonest individuals cross our paths, people for whom gratitude feels impossible. After years of practicing gratitude, I still had two people I despised; their very names triggered tension in my body. A peer coach suggested an exercise: write their names and grievances daily for a week. I did. To my surprise, I discovered that part of my frustration was my own silence; I was resisting speaking up.

I still disagree with their behavior, but I no longer cringe. I speak up respectfully, set boundaries, and view them as humans with poor behaviors rather than villains. Gratitude revealed my growth edge and compassion.

Negativity comes in many shades, biases, people, and cultures. While gratitude doesn't erase negativity, it creates space for truth, tolerance, change, and even empathy. It reminds us to see people first, behaviors second, and as Truth #1 reminds us, to anchor ourselves in resilience when negativity strikes. **Why this matters to leaders** is that reducing and removing negativity improves engagement, retention, and innovation.

Confronting Negativity Takeaways

- Negative people and cultures are draining and difficult to stay grateful around.
- Strengthening gratitude when in negative situations.
- Consciously model grateful behaviors.
- Changing a negative person or workplace is very difficult.
- You can't change negative people unless they want to change; gratitude keeps leaders from joining their negativity.
- Examining people you despise through gratitude can teach you about yourself.
- You can complain gratefully and in the service of truth-telling and get results.

Reflection Questions

1. What is your typical response to negative people?

2. How might you use gratitude to respond to negativity?

3. What beliefs do you have about negative people, cultures, and change?

Chapter 15
Forcing and Faking Gratitude

*Reality is that which, when you stop believing in it,
doesn't go away.*
~ Philip K. Dick, author

I was once labeled a pushover, too nice, too quiet, even a Pollyanna. I had a deeply ingrained habit of forcing myself to feel gratitude. This habit narrowed my view of reality to only the slices I could handle. It was a form of denial. I had to learn to cultivate genuine gratitude.

Gratitude isn't a switch you flip; it's a drip that nourishes. Forced gratitude kept me stuck, with no real progress or growth. Whether forcing gratitude occurs consciously or unconsciously, its primary impact is the same: we avoid seeing the whole truth and delay addressing all the problems or discomfort.

In my case, forcing gratitude was both a mindset and a habit. I believed (mindset) that positivity alone could make any issue vanish, and things would be better. Over the years, that habit became deeply embedded as a form of "gratitude abuse" that eroded confidence and trust in myself and my teams. This was one of my biggest gratitude challenges and the hardest to overcome.

My Wake-Up Call

I grew up with a nice mother who never said anything negative about anyone. Because I learned not to speak up, I didn't handle conflict well. So, I first chose a career where I could hide in a cubicle and make a good living, software engineering. It was a career that I thought would allow me to keep to myself and avoid any conflict. A more logical and less emotional career. However, I wasn't a very good software engineer, and I was more interested in teaching and translation; translating the work of the geniuses around me into meaningful and usable products. I was very proud of my logical engineering background; I assumed I saw reality clearly. It wasn't until years later, while in the role of senior engineering director, that a 360-degree leadership feedback assessment of me shattered that illusion. At the time, I led a team of over 100 professionals, with a dozen managers and directors reporting to me. The team, which developed software networking products, generated sales of over half a billion dollars in the late '90s.

When the feedback arrived, it felt brutal and eye-opening. Twenty-five years later, I still have a well-worn paper copy of that report. It revealed how my niceness, rooted in forced gratitude, held my team and me back: conflicts went unaddressed, misplaced trust was rampant, and I smiled and agreed when I shouldn't have. I had to learn how to speak hard truths in a kind way.

With this awareness as my compass, I set out to undo years of forced gratitude.

Reversing the Habit and Be More Grateful

Over time, I reversed my habit of forcing gratitude and discovered genuine gratitude on the other side. Change began with awareness: seeing myself clearly, practicing mindfulness, and giving and receiving honest feedback. From there, trial and error led to solutions that stuck. Here's some of what I learned and tried to overcome my habit of forced gratitude.

Mindfulness

Paying attention to the present moment without judgment builds self-awareness. I resisted meditation for years, even after sampling many modalities. Only after completing an eight-week Mind-Body Stress Reduction (MBSR) workshop, based on the work of John Kabat-Zinn, did I become a regular meditator.

This practice sharpened my ability to notice when I am slipping into forced gratitude. **Takeaway:** Build mindfulness to be more self-aware.

Ask for Feedback, Regularly
Cultivate the habit of inviting and accepting feedback. Kim Scott, in her book *Radical Candor*, recounts how Sheryl Sandberg pressed for specific reactions after a presentation until Kim offered an honest and helpful critique. Ask, give permission, keep probing, get specific, then thank the giver. One courageous leader I coached even crowd-sourced her own feedback on Facebook, proof that seeking input is a gift, though not a strategy for everyone. **Takeaway:** Invite regular feedback to uncover blind spots.

Master Constructive Feedback Techniques
There are so many techniques for giving feedback; to help you find one that works for you, here's a sampling:
- Radical Candor = kind and clear
- Sandwich method = praise → critique → praise
- SBI = Situation-Behavior-Impact
- BOOST Model = Balanced, Objective, Observed, Specific, Timely
- AID Model = Action-Impact-Desired Behavior
- Marshall Goldsmith's Feed-Forward Technique

And it will still be hard regardless of what technique you use. A leader I coached practiced giving feedback in everyday scenarios, such as complaining about a supermarket scale that was inaccurate or an airline delay. It became enjoyable hearing about her different feedback approaches and troubleshooting them to deal with inequity and unfairness in the world during each coaching meeting. The world outside work became her feedback technique testbed. Over time, those small moments built her confidence and clarity. She got so good at it that she could have become a consumer advocate. **Takeaway:** Practice purposeful feedback to hone clarity and honesty.

Complain without Whining

Complaining, truth-telling in the service of improvement, differs from whining. Fran Lebowitz, author, social commentator, and public speaker, describes whining as unacceptable noise, whereas a justified complaint can spark change. Complaints paired with gratitude and aimed at betterment carry real power. **Takeaway:** Use constructive complaints to spark real improvement.

Practice Being Negative

During coach certification, a master coach challenged me to name three things I disliked each day in my gratitude journal. At first, it felt odd, but over the years, I have learned that passing judgment and allowing negativity can clear the path for understanding. It helps me gain insight into myself, my core beliefs, and room for gratitude.

Takeaway: Practice naming dislikes to build self-clarity.

Gamify Your Principles

I love games. I invented a "Three Strikes" rule: forgive the first two offenses, then act on the third. In my personal life, the third time my ex-husband cheated, I asked for a divorce. In business, when a client's no-show without notice occurs three times, I let them go kindly. **Takeaway:** Gamify your principles to create actionable habits.

Replace Trigger Phrases

"I'm fine" used to be my automatic deflection, signaling "don't ask" or "stop talking." Now I choose honest alternatives:

- "Thank you for being here."
- "I'm not ready to discuss that yet."
- "Yes, I hear you."
- Simple gestures, a nod, eye contact, to acknowledge without pretending.

Takeaway: Replace trite phrases with ones that encourage honest acknowledgment.

Cultivate Emotional Intelligence

Self-awareness, one of the cornerstones of emotional intelligence, helps you spot when you're forcing gratitude and ignoring your feelings.

Takeaway: Build Emotional intelligence to strengthen self-awareness and recognize genuine gratitude.

Is Forced Gratitude Ever Acceptable?

In service roles, staff often recite gratitude scripts that aim to evoke positive emotions in customers. If sincere, it can be delightful, and the customer is more open to purchasing; if hollow, it may feel insincere. A recent phone-service interaction I had somehow felt authentic when the agent said, "We appreciate you being a customer for twenty-five years, a SMART gratitude moment, specific and meaningful. I didn't know I had been a customer for 25 years, and her delivery seemed genuine, yet I knew it was part of the script.

Forced gratitude lives in gray areas, shaped by beliefs and ethics. With social norms pressing us toward quick positivity, it's easy to slip into forced gratitude in moments of deep pain.

Consider going to a funeral for the first time as an adult, one where you are not familiar with the traditions or culture. Going to a funeral is difficult, regardless. Each culture has different traditions. Not knowing what to do or say stops some people from reaching out or attending a funeral because it's uncomfortable. They may not go because they don't know what's expected, they want to avoid the unknown or negative emotions of grief, anger, or sadness. If they attend, they may say things to the grieving that are harmful because they want to make them feel better. They might say things like, "Time will heal," or "At least you had many good years together." The intention behind the statements may be from a compassionate place, wanting to make the other person feel better or lessen the blow. And saying these types of phrases when you don't mean them could be a learned cultural response to make them or you feel better. Yet, many times, it's forcing gratitude because we don't know any other way.

In the workplace, after a major system outage, leaders might say, "I'm grateful we all pulled through," without acknowledging the long hours or frustration, a forced rush to positivity that sows distrust because the long hours worked are not recognized.

Instead of forcing gratitude, try expressing it through simple words that express what is present now, embrace silence, or use actions. From a place of drip-like authenticity, you can say, "I'm sorry for your loss. I'm here for you." You can ask, "What help do you need now?" or offer specific help. When my ex-husband passed away over twenty years ago, I still appreciate and am grateful to the people who vacuumed the rugs, organized the food donations, and our neighbors, who gave us Red Sox tickets a week after he died.

Responding to Others' Forced Gratitude

Now that I'm a recovered gratitude-forcer, I notice it in others. Depending on the situation, you can choose to ask gentle questions, call attention to the gap, or let it pass.

What this means for you as a leader is that when you can spot force or fake gratitude, it is sowing the seeds of mistrust and misunderstanding, and you now have an opportunity to change that.

Forcing and Faking Gratitude Takeaways

- People force gratitude for many reasons, often unconsciously.
- Forced gratitude erodes trust and hides reality.
- Depending on context and intent, it can seem manipulative or socially acceptable.
- Unlearning forced gratitude requires a new mindset and new behaviors.
- Some areas to grow in that will help are feedback skills, constructive complaints, gamification, trigger-word replacement, and emotional intelligence.

Reflection Questions

1. Recall a recent moment when you offered gratitude by habit rather than feeling it. What triggered that response, and how could you pause to be more genuine next time?

2. Which strategy (mindfulness, feedback-seeking, constructive complaining, gamification, trigger-phrase swaps) do you already do or might try?

3. Identify a relationship where you dodge hard conversations. How will you speak an uncomfortable truth kindly?

Chapter 16
Gratitude Translation Errors

True communication isn't what you say. It's what the receiver takes away.
~ Tom Monahan, American entrepreneur

Gratitude isn't limited by age, culture, politics, or gender; it's universal. Like Dr. Seuss's Sneetches, it is foolish to judge who 'has it' and who doesn't. Gratitude can be invisible or visible, expressed through thoughts, behaviors, attitudes, and actions.

The misunderstanding of who is grateful and who is not often begins with assumptions and judgments due to how gratitude is communicated and expressed. You can substitute your favorite disliked person or misunderstood group for the Sneetches, and you have a common gratitude challenge. Just because someone expresses gratitude differently from you doesn't mean they are not grateful. Just because someone doesn't seem grateful doesn't mean they aren't.

Miscommunication about gratitude can limit the impact a leader can have. You can practice gratitude deeply, yet if you don't know how to express it to different audiences, your intention may fall flat or worse, be received as boastful, self-serving, or political. The more diverse your workplace, the more likely translation errors are to occur.

A Generational Misfire

A Baby Boomer leader once organized a large donation to a charity to thank her team. She imagined confetti and applause; instead, her mostly Millennial staff felt overlooked and were unimpressed. They wanted personal acknowledgment, not a public gesture that felt boastful and out of touch.

When "Thank You" Goes Astray

Even a simple "thank you" can misfire in a multinational setting. The British say "thank you" more than any other nationality. In contrast, among Lao speakers in Southeast Asia or Siwu speakers in Western Africa, saying "thank you" is so rare it can feel awkward or even bizarre.

Unraveling our own and others' beliefs about gratitude is a complex process. But because gratitude is a strategic skill for leaders (see Truth #2), it's essential to learn these differences and adapt our expressions to convey genuine appreciation.

Clues for Gratitude Translation

Below are categories that influence how people give and receive gratitude. Use them as a starting point for solving gratitude translation errors:

- Gender
- Age
- Disability
- Family-of-origin culture
- National, local, and community cultures
- Workplace cultures
- Personality, both innate and learned
- Past experiences
- Sneetches with stars on their bellies

These categories are generalizations, not rules. Everyone's experience is unique, but these clues help leaders adapt their approach and avoid misfires.

From Theory to Practice

In my previous book, *Leading with Gratitude*, I explore cultural and personality differences through Hofstede's Cultural Dimensions, DiSC styles, and statistical research. In this book, I take a personal and practical approach, showing you how to bridge the gaps in real time.

Language, Accents, and Class

In the mid-1930s, George and Ira Gershwin captured linguistic divides in "Let's Call the Whole Thing Off," made famous by Ella Fitzgerald:

> You like potato and I like potahto
> You like tomato and I like tomahto
> Potato, potahto, tomato, tomahto
> Let's call the whole thing off

The difference in pronunciation can be regional, cultural, or signal class differences, as in this song. At the time of this song, these pronunciations were considered less refined by the upper class. People make assumptions and generalizations when they hear accents or word usage. I know people who adjust their dialect and word usage according to the person they are interacting with. Today, accents still trigger assumptions like these, that people have said to me:

- "She talks that way, so I'll tip her less."
- "He's smart because of his accent, so I appreciate his work more."
- "They sound ungrateful because of how they speak."

Leaders who understand the differences and, when appropriate, shift their dialect or word choice to match their audience show cultural fluency and respect.

Gender Roles, Sexual Identity, and Gratitude

Gender roles and individual beliefs about gender roles run the gamut. It can be challenging to keep up with the latest acceptable phrasing, as it evolves. To my grandparents, 'gay' never meant anything other than carefree and happy. Gender roles can be traditional, unconventional, and fluid. Sadly, I've seen that those who don't conform to whatever traditional understanding of any of the categories listed above in the current timeframe, including Sneetches, may face overt or covert discrimination. Discrimination impacts a person's overall well-being. It's hard to be grateful when our beliefs and sense of self are not accepted or validated. It can make people fearful and withdrawn. When people are not accepted for who they are, many don't do their best work and may operate from fear, which may also cause them to leave, rebel, or fight. A grateful workplace accepts people for who they are, regardless of any category, and those who don't conform.

A Generational Tour of Gratitude

"Thank you is overused and not meaningful," my Millennial stepson told me. I am at the tail end of the Baby Boomers and was taught to say 'thank you' often. This contradicts the generations of my father and grandfather, the Greatest Generation (my dad) and the Silent Generation (my grandfather), as well as my children's generation, the Millennials. My father rarely said thank you. When he did, it was well thought out, generally in private, and he would wait for the right moment. He meant it sincerely, yet it scared me because it was so unusual, since he used the same tone and method for reprimands.

Here's a summary of the stereotypical generational approach to gratitude.

Across eras, gratitude reflects the core values and challenges of each generation. While methods differ, the underlying appreciation for people and opportunity is universal.

The Silent & Greatest Generations (1901–1945)
Context: World Wars, the Depression, radio, and print media.
Expression: They gave lots quietly but said less. When they do talk, they are deliberate about gratitude and make it a point to speak it out loud. They will express gratitude through loyalty and actions, sending thank-you notes and personal gestures that reinforce relationships.

Baby Boomers (1946–1964)

Context: Post-war prosperity, social change, television's rise.

Expression: Public acknowledgment, material gifts, charitable donations. Television started to become a strong influencer for Baby Boomers; shows like *I Love Lucy*, *Leave It to Beaver*, and *Star Trek* became cultural icons of the time.

Generation X (1965–1980)

Context: Economic uncertainty, feminism's rise, analog-to-digital transition.

Expression: Pragmatic, individualistic; gratitude through experiences and quality time. Xers value work-life balance and may offer a quiet "thank you" over grand gestures. The AIDS health epidemic was new, and at its peak, pervasive consumer technology was stabilizing, and feminism was taking hold. They are sometimes called the middle child and are used to change, and they adapt to Baby Boomers and Millennials. They are more skeptical and cynical, but they still appreciate the things they have. Sarcastic television shows like *Friends* and *The Simpsons* shaped them.

Millennials (1981–1996)

Context: Connected technology, diversity, gig economy.

Expression: Diverse handwritten notes, social media shout-outs, volunteering. In the United States, they are the most racially and ethnically diverse group. They are comfortable with technology. They are entrepreneurial. They are socially conscious, and many have delayed or changed traditional societal norms of marriage and having children. They are social media- and stream-savvy. Because they are so diverse, their favorite podcasts, television/movies, and social media habits vary. Even with my three millennial sons, their social media consumption ranges dramatically from conservative to liberal to over-the-top sports, reality television, and How-to YouTube videos. One son has no social media presence, another has a minimal one, and the last one has a full-blown professional media presence.

Generation Z (1997-2012)
Context: True digital natives, authenticity seekers.
Expression: Memes, GIFs, video messages, digital gift cards, short, transparent, heartfelt.

Generation Alpha (2012-present)
Context: Born into voice assistants and tablets. Their lives are fully recorded.
Expression: Still emerging, but likely hyper-digital and immediacy-driven.

I remain hopeful: By learning to understand, we can bridge these gaps, and leaders can translate their gratitude to any audience. The universal thread is clear: people want to feel seen, valued, and understood, regardless of how they express and say, "thank you.

Summary

Like the Sneetches, we all carry assumptions that can quietly block the giving and receiving of gratitude. The way gratitude is given and received is unique for each individual and sometimes can be predicted by their age, personality, or culture, but not always. Translation errors remind us that while gratitude is simple in principle, it is often complex in practice.

What this means is that leaders who remain curious and adaptable in their approach to giving gratitude ensure that it can be genuinely received and not misinterpreted.

Gratitude Translation Errors Takeaways

- Gratitude is universal, yet its expression is not. Miscommunication happens when leaders assume other people experience or value gratitude the same way they do.
- Translation errors limit impact. A heartfelt gesture can backfire when it clashes with cultural, generational, or personal expectations.
- Generational and cultural lenses shape gratitude. From handwritten notes to memes, each group has distinct norms that influence how they show and receive thanks.
- Invisible doesn't mean absent. Just because someone doesn't verbalize gratitude doesn't mean they don't feel or value it.
- Leaders need gratitude-cultural fluency. Adjusting language, gestures, and approaches shows respect and ensures that gratitude is received as intended.
- Gratitude evolves. As norms change and workplaces become more diverse, leaders must remain curious and adaptable in expressing and communicating gratitude.

Reflection Questions

1. What categories (age, culture, personality, etc.) shape gratitude in your team, and how will you adapt your expressions to connect with each person?

2. Which generational or cultural gratitude style challenges you most, and what one action will you take this week to bridge that gap?

3. Reflect on a recent "gratitude misfire" you observed or experienced. How would you reframe it to ensure the receiver truly feels appreciated?

Chapter 17
Redefining Giving

*Feeling gratitude and not expressing it is like
wrapping a present and not giving it.
~ William Arthur Ward, author*

Bake sales, corporate giving drives, charity auctions, on the surface, these seem like simple ways to show support and build community. Yet when participation feels mandatory, gratitude can quickly turn into a sense of obligation. Cookies, charities, and choice may seem unrelated, but together they reveal how giving, done with clear expectations and genuine appreciation, can either strengthen or strain workplaces.

"I suppose I could have stayed home, baked cookies, and had teas," said Hillary Clinton in 1992.

Regardless of your personal opinions about Hillary Clinton, those words ignited a firestorm of backlash. At the time, Clinton was a married professional woman and full-time working mother, a reality far less common or accepted in 1992 than it is now. Clinton had the means to stay home and bake cookies, yet she chose not to.

At the time, when Clinton made that remark, I was also a professional woman, working in the male-dominated field of technology. We were one of the first generations of women who were told we could have it all and didn't have many role models to show us how to do it, have a career, be a leader, and raise children. For me, staying home and baking cookies wasn't an option; I needed an income. Yet, in the suburb where I lived, the traditional expectation for a middle-class white woman was still to stay home as a full-time housewife. Nationally, the trend was shifting, but in my immediate world, I was an outlier.

At that time, many of the moms around me spent hours baking and hosting bake sales. That was considered the "right" way to show up and contribute. I didn't bake, and frankly, you probably wouldn't have wanted to eat anything I made. I couldn't understand the economics: spending $6 on ingredients and four hours of labor to raise a few hundred dollars across dozens of bakers. *It would have been easier to write a check.*

At that time, I was in the rare three percent of women in the United States earning over $100,000 a year. At my hourly rate, those four hours of cookie labor meant I was losing money.

So, yes, I was an anti-bake-*sale mom*. It was an unpopular and controversial position in my community, so I kept my thoughts  to myself. I believed in the causes and wanted to support them, just not by baking. Instead, I did other things, including buying cookies from the bake sales.

While all this was happening in my personal life, I was also a senior director at a billion-dollar tech company. One of the company's giving initiatives was an annual push to donate to the corporation's chosen charity.

Managers were pressured to encourage their employees to give, and as a director, I was expected to lead the charge. Like the bake sale, I didn't dislike the cause; I simply didn't believe in pressuring people to give to an organization that didn't always support their beliefs.

Bake sales, I realized, are a lot like corporate giving programs. Whether it's cookies or donations, the underlying message can be: *If you want to fit in, you have to give, this way.* Creating that sense of mandatory giving, even when unspoken, can backfire. It forces people into a narrow definition of contribution, which often breeds resentment rather than genuine gratitude.

These programs are typically created to inspire generosity and bring people together. Yet not everyone knows how to decline or set boundaries and still feel like they belong. That's where leaders and cultures have a choice. Leaders can learn to create giving programs that genuinely make people feel grateful in a way that resonates with each individual.

When "No" Isn't an Option

Many people struggle to say no for various reasons, including fear of not fitting in, lack of conviction in the cause, or concern that they'll be socially ostracized or even fired.

A former Disney employee shared with me that in their culture, they were not allowed to say "no." Instead, they learned to soften their refusals by using humor, making a funny noise, or offering alternatives. Authentic alternatives to "no" might sound like:

- *I'm honored you asked.*
- *Is there something else I can do to help?*
- *Could we try an alternative?*
- *I might know someone who could help.*
- *Would you be willing to chat more about this?*

- *I'm booked this month; could you ask again later?*

Simple phrases like these respect both the request and the boundaries.

When Giving Becomes a Chore

Sometimes giving stops feeling good and starts feeling like an obligation. I remember one mom who stayed up until the wee hours of the morning to finish baking. Instead of feeling grateful, she felt resentment.

As leaders, we need to pay attention to signs like this. Acknowledge individual effort in a way that genuinely fits the person, not just the task.

Setting Clear Expectations

Another time, a bake sale committee expected more cookies than someone delivered, and they reacted with anger. That baker never volunteered again.

Clear expectations make all the difference. Leaders should communicate expectations upfront, how much is needed, what type, by when, and how it should be packaged. For example:

Can you bake three dozen cookies of your choice, individually wrapped, and deliver them here by Friday? It may take about four hours of your time.

When Effort Isn't Appreciated

Sometimes the cookies simply don't taste good. Gossip starts. "She's a terrible baker" becomes "She's terrible at her job." Gratitude disappears, and the giver doesn't feel appreciated.

In moments like this, leaders have two jobs:
1. Shut down the gossip.
2. If appropriate, gently address the issue directly with the giver.

The gratitude belongs in acknowledging the effort, not tearing down the attempt.

Inappropriate or Unclear Guidelines

Another example: cookies with nuts. They got thrown out. The baker, who had worked hard, felt dismissed.

This ties back to overcommunication, what I call the *broken record of clarity*. State expectations multiple times, both in writing and verbally, so everyone is clear about what is required.

Done "Wrong" or Not Perfect

I recall volunteers who were informed that they had priced the cookies incorrectly. Each person had their logic, considering the cost of ingredients, advice from friends, and personal judgment. None of them were wrong, just different.

My friend spent hours driving around town hanging up bake-sale signs she had made. The signs were not perfectly centered, so another volunteer took them down and redid them. My friend didn't feel appreciated at all, even though she had done the job well enough for most people. Focusing on the why, not obsessing over the how, would have made all the difference. These examples remind leaders that perfection is less important than participation. When we value effort over outcome, we create workplaces where people feel safe contributing in their own way. Appreciate the person and the effort, even if the result isn't flawless. Humor and lightheartedness help, too.

Bake Sales, Giving Programs, and Gratitude

Bake sales and workplace giving programs are meant to foster appreciation and support meaningful causes. Yet when they feel mandatory or tied to job performance, they can have the opposite effect.

When done right, giving programs can:
- Bring people together for a common cause.
- Build gratitude within teams.
- Help people feel good about contributing.
- Highlight causes that deserve attention.

And this isn't small work. According to *The Chronicle of Philanthropy*, foundations and charities gave an estimated $557.16 billion to U.S. charities in 2023 alone. That's a lot of giving along with a lot of potential for gratitude or frustration, depending on how it's handled.

Why this matters to leaders is that, regardless of good intentions, giving can seriously go wrong, demoralizing and disengaging people in the workplace. Regardless of whether it's a bake sale or a corporate initiative, start with purpose and gratitude.

Recognize that people give differently, time, money, creativity, and honor their choice. Above all, appreciate the person and the effort, not just the outcome.

Redefining Giving Takeaways

- Giving should inspire, not obligate.
- Clear communication and realistic expectations prevent resentment.
- Gratitude belongs to recognizing effort, not perfection.
- Offering options honors individual styles of giving and receiving.
- Focus on the why, the results, and purpose, not how someone does it (unless legal or safety concerns).
- Leaders set the tone: model appreciation, shut down gossip, and keep expectations visible.

Reflection Questions

1. How do you decline respectfully and gratefully when someone asks you to give?

2. What giving programs are needed or need to be modified where you work?

3. How do you ensure that giving programs are inclusive of all and don't backfire?

Chapter 18
Gratitude Limiting Beliefs

If you want small changes, work on your behavior; if you want quantum leap changes, work on your paradigms.
~ Stephen R. Covey, author

According to Stephen Covey, a paradigm is a mental map, a framework of beliefs, often deeply rooted in our background and experiences. Mental frameworks shape how we behave in the world.

Our gratitude-limiting beliefs often feel invisible, as if they are simply who we are. Yet they drive our choices, shape our mindset, and influence our habits, behaviors, and actions. The longer we hold them, the harder they are to see or change.

Yet when we do challenge and shift these deepest beliefs, that's when the most significant transformations happen. By creating a new paradigm, a framework sometimes makes new behaviors and assumptions appear easily. We see reality differently.

Changing a limiting belief can unlock new energy, clarity, and gratitude in ways we didn't expect.

Even leaders who are known for their gratitude continually work on these beliefs. The most common belief I hear from already grateful leaders is that they are *"already grateful enough."* Beliefs often hide in plain sight because they are such a core part of who we are. They can be helpful, neutral, or limiting, and the goal is to uncover the ones that quietly block us from growing in gratitude.

Common Gratitude-Limiting Beliefs
Below is a list I've gathered from my research and work with leaders over the past six years. A leader spoke each phrase, limiting their ability to strengthen gratitude. You might recognize yourself or someone on your team in these five categories of examples:

Self-Perception & Vulnerability
- Grateful Enough – "I'm a very grateful person; I don't understand why…"
- Fear of Vulnerability – "Gratitude makes me weak or vulnerable."
- Too Soft or Kind – "People think I'm a pushover and will walk all over me because I'm grateful."
- Gratitude Is Passive – "Gratitude is a feeling, not an active practice that requires effort."
- Gratitude Is Selfish – "If I focus on my gratitude, I'm not helping others."

Scarcity, Time, and Overwhelm

- Scarcity – "I don't have enough; how can I be grateful?"
- Gratitude Is a Luxury – "I must pay the bill first."
- Overwhelmed and No Time – "I have too many problems already and no time."
- Focus on the Future – "I'll be grateful when I get that raise, job, money, or a good boss…"

Perfectionism & Unrealistic Expectations

- Perfectionism – "Things are only worth appreciating if they are perfect."
- Unrealistic Expectations – "Life should be better than this."
- Too Big – "Gratitude is only for the big things in life, like birthdays and holidays."

Negativity & Habit Loops

- Negativity Bias – "Bad things outweigh the good things."
- Habitual Complaining – "It's easier to focus on what's wrong."
- Comparison with Others – "Others have it better than me."

Materialism & Entitlement

- Materialism – "Things are more important, and I can't appreciate anything without at least…"
- Entitlement – "I deserve more than this."

- Competitive and Outcome Focused – "Achieving and winning is more important."

Past Trauma
- Past Trauma – "I need to resolve my trauma before I can focus on being grateful."

You may notice overlaps in gratitude-limiting beliefs.

These are statements from real individuals expressed in their own way. To them, these statements have real and sometimes profound meaning. If one belief resonates with you but the wording isn't quite right, rephrase it in your own words so that you can better find an alternative belief that supports gratitude strengthening.

Why Beliefs Are So Powerful
Beliefs are embedded in individuals and workplaces. They quietly shape culture, decisions, and day-to-day interactions. That's why organizational visions, missions, and values can be powerful when applied. They're collective attempts to replace limiting beliefs with empowering ones.

As James Clear, author of *Atomic Habits*, points out, beliefs are tied to belonging:
Convincing someone to change their mind is really the process of convincing them to change their tribe. If they abandon their beliefs, they run the risk of losing

social ties. You can't expect someone to change their mind if you take away their community, too. You have to give them somewhere to go. Nobody wants their worldview torn apart if loneliness is the outcome.

In workplaces, this means shifting a gratitude-limiting belief can feel like losing your community, unless leaders create new, supportive beliefs and environments.

Replacing Limiting Beliefs

Once you spot a gratitude-limiting belief, the key is to experiment with a replacement that feels believable. Here are a few examples leaders have found helpful:

Limiting Belief	Suggested Replacement Belief
I'm grateful enough.	Gratitude can always be stronger.
Being grateful will make me a pushover and too nice.	You can be grateful and powerful and say difficult things.
I don't have enough time to practice gratitude.	It only takes 30 seconds. It's everywhere. I can always find something to be grateful for.

Belief awareness about gratitude and learning to change those beliefs should be a regular part of your gratitude practice, something you return to again and again. Think of beliefs as a house of cards: once one limiting belief topples, others start to shift as well. Toppling the negative core limiting belief allows room for a new set of gratitude-supporting beliefs to be built on a firmer foundation.

Helping Your Team Shift Gratitude-Limiting Beliefs Model vulnerability.
Share one of your own gratitude-limiting beliefs and how you're working to shift it. When leaders go first, it creates a sense of safety for others to explore their own beliefs.

Create safe conversations.
Hold small group discussions or one-on-ones where team members can discuss what gets in the way of expressing gratitude. Emphasize that there are no "wrong" beliefs, only opportunities to grow.

Weave Gratitude into Purpose.
Some workplaces weave gratitude directly into their mission, vision, or values. Here are examples:

Generic: "Our team vision is to serve with excellence, compassion, and gratitude, recognizing every contribution and every person we meet."

Southwest Airlines: "We work with a **Servant's Heart**: putting others first and showing **gratitude**, caring, and compassion." (Source: Southwest Airlines Culture & Values)

The Random Acts of Flowers Mission (Knoxville, Tennessee, USA): "To improve the emotional health and well-being of individuals in health care facilities by delivering recycled flowers, encouragement, and personal moments of kindness. We cultivate a culture of compassion and gratitude through volunteerism." (Source: Random Acts of Flowers official site)

Connect belief shifts to purpose.
Link the practice of gratitude back to your team's vision or mission. When people see how gratitude supports meaningful work, it's easier to let go of old beliefs.

Celebrate small shifts.
When someone demonstrates a new gratitude-supporting belief (for example, noticing effort rather than perfection), call it out and thank them. Small acknowledgments reinforce new mindsets.

Offer an alternative "tribe."
As James Clear notes, changing beliefs often means finding new social anchors. Foster a team culture where gratitude is normal for everyday and still appreciated, so people feel they belong as they grow.

Beliefs shape what we notice, value, and practice. Shift even one toward gratitude, and you transform how you lead, connect, and live.

Gratitude Limiting Beliefs Takeaways

- Shifting our beliefs, that's when the most significant transformations happen.
- It is challenging to see our own beliefs because they are deeply ingrained and invisible.
- There are many types of gratitude-limiting beliefs that are unique to individuals.
- Discover how to replace a limiting belief with gratitude, thereby strengthening it.
- Leaders can integrate and weave gratitude into purpose to show these beliefs in action.

Reflection Questions

1. Write down your beliefs about gratitude and notice if they limit or support you in having more gratitude.

2. What is the impact of your beliefs about gratitude?

3. Notice and ask about others' gratitude beliefs in your workplace, what impact do they have on culture and connection?

PART V
Living the Gratitude Way
Transforming leaders, teams, and workplaces

Taking Action

This final part brings everything together with practical frameworks and tools, guiding you to move from insight to action to close the gratitude gap. It will help you make gratitude a lived, daily leadership practice.

Act with gratitude, and you will create a ripple of change around you.

It's Time to Rock and Roll

Chapter 19
Gratitude Practice Framework

Your beliefs become your thoughts,
Your thoughts become your words,
Your words become your actions,
Your actions become your habits,
Your habits become your values,
Your values become your destiny.
~ Mahatma Gandhi

This famous sequence from Gandhi applies directly to gratitude: when gratitude becomes a habit, it shapes your values and, ultimately, your destiny.

What gets measured gets managed.
~ Peter Drucker, International Business Consultant

And as Peter Drucker reminds us, to make something real, you need to be able to measure it. Drucker valued measurement as a tool for focus and accountability, yet warned against its overuse or misuse. He wanted leaders to ask: *"Are we measuring what really matters?"* Gratitude is not a short-term metric; it is a critical foundational skill that matters for building sustainable workplaces that achieve success.

Gratitude, like any critical skill, has a better chance of thriving when you measure and manage it intentionally and purposefully. It's not a 'do it once and forget it' approach. The most successful practices are those that are continually refined and adapted as success is achieved and changes occur.

Why Practice Intentionally?
Despite the common advice to keep a gratitude journal, it's not the only way to practice gratitude, and if you don't enjoy writing, you likely won't stick with it.

Even after twenty years of journaling, I've found myself getting bored writing "I'm grateful for my dog" over and over. The key is to find a method that improves your and your workplace's gratitude baseline measurement.

In this chapter, I introduce a simple yet powerful framework for creating a successful gratitude practice tailored to your needs. We'll also examine how this framework can be applied in the workplace.

Today, you operate from a certain gratitude baseline, which is your current level of gratitude, whether or not you've measured it. Everyone's baseline is different, shaped by many factors such as DNA, experiences, culture, and gender. You have a choice: keep it where it is or deliberately strengthen and move it forward.

The framework has three parts:
1. **Goal (Vision/Why)** – why you want to strengthen your gratitude, your purpose, your reasons.
2. **Plan (What, How, When)** – a realistic plan you'll follow consistently.
3. **Do (Act and Adjust)** – putting your plan into action and refining as you go.

Insights from Experts

Experts offer varied perspectives on what constitutes an effective practice. Here are two leading voices on the science of gratitude.

Dr. Robert Emmons suggests:
- Keep a gratitude journal
- Count your blessings
- Compare your current situations
- Use concrete reminders
- Practice mindfulness

Dr. Andrew Huberman suggests:
- *Only five minutes, three times a week,* is enough to start
- Ground it in a story you can emotionally relate to
- "It can even be the bullet points of the story."

Real-World Examples

These practices come from leaders I've interviewed. They show how gratitude can fit into many different lives and schedules:

Amanda - Morning & Evening Routine: A busy nurse practitioner who uses the 5-Minute Journal each morning and evening.

Suzan - Active Gratitude: A corporate marketing consultant who tracks *active gratitude*, what she did, not just what happened.

Marie - Gratitude in Motion: An executive coach and minister who says what she's grateful for aloud while holding a plank.

Jeanne - 1:1 Appreciation: A technology VP who ends every 1:1 meeting by telling the other person one thing she appreciates about them.

Sonya - In Every Conversation: A mortgage lender who intentionally states something she appreciates in every conversation.

Peter - Meeting Openers: A wastewater business development manager who starts every meeting with appreciation for a person, company, or situation.

My practice: I've kept a gratitude journal for over twenty-five years, experimenting with prompts and techniques as new challenges arise.

The Gratitude Practice Framework: Goal, Plan, Do
Based on decades of experience as a project/program manager, leader, coach, and teacher of project management and leadership, I offer this simple and powerful three-step framework, which is based on tried-and-true methodologies.

Step 1: Goal (Vision/Why)
Determine and Clarify Your Why
Your Why is your purpose, your reason to practice gratitude. It guides every decision you make, and the more connected you are to it, the easier and more powerful your practice becomes.

Sample Whys:
- To be a better leader
- To create positive workplaces
- To bring gratitude into my daily life as unconscious habits
- To be healthier physically, mentally, and socially
- To be engaged and innovative
- To make better decisions
- To build stronger relationships
- To enjoy life and work more

Refine Your Why into Specific Goals:

- Complete all the Reflection Questions in this book and look for patterns.
- Review your gratitude challenges and prioritize them.
- Ask a trusted peer for feedback on your gratitude behaviors.
- Research leaders or ask mentors about their gratitude goals and practices.

Most leaders start with a mindset: challenging beliefs and learning to do the 3-step shift to gratitude.

Step 2: Plan (What, How, When)
Pick and Create Steps, Strategies, Tactics, Habits, and Processes to Support Your Why

Your plan is how you'll achieve your Why. It breaks down your why, your purpose, and your concise goals into actionable, achievable goals with specific methods and timelines. It could be a set of steps or processes that will change your habits and behaviors.

Example:

Why: To be a better leader.

Plan: In every 1:1 meeting with my direct report, share one thing I'm grateful for and ask how I can assist them. If no 1:1s occur, ensure that communication happens at least weekly.

Do: Implement this for thirty days, then adjust as needed.

Gratitude Practice Framework

Start with a General Practice:
- How often: daily, three times a week, weekly
- How long: five to ten minutes, one hour
- Activity: choose one that activates your gratitude

Examples:
- Morning and evening: write down three to five things you're grateful for
- Complete one page of a 5-Minute Gratitude Journal each day
- Dance to happy music while thinking about what you're grateful for
- Pair gratitude practice with daily actions like brushing teeth, showering, driving
- Begin planning sessions by saying aloud what you're grateful for
- Once a week, tell someone you appreciate them

Personalize Your Practice:
- Take a gratitude assessment
- List and prioritize your practice goals, focusing on those that support your Why
- Target areas like consistency, depth, mindset, habits, or specific challenges

Build Checkpoints into Your Plan:
- Review at least yearly
- Ideally review every 3-4 months (or at anchor points like birthdays, new seasons)

Step 3: Do (Act and Adjust)
Move to Action
Execute your plan.
- Check in on milestones regularly
- Create a habit tracker
- Find an accountability buddy
- Adjust and forgive, everything is a lesson
- Focus on gains
- Adjust to make it work for your environment

Daily "Live It" Questions:
The technique I use daily, borrowed from Agile Project Management, is the three-question stand-up meeting format, adapted.
1. Why am I doing this? What is my goal?
2. What did I do yesterday, and what lesson did I learn?
3. What will I do today?

Adjust as Needed
Revisit and adjust your practice based on asking these questions regularly.

Will it **strengthen** your gratitude?
- Find a way to measure it, use your baseline tool or anecdotal evidence.
- Example: *"I'm no longer angry when I'm stuck in traffic."*
- Simple metric: *"How many times this week did I thank someone in a meeting?"*

Does your practice **activate** your gratitude?
- Does it make you feel grateful, not just think about being grateful?

Have you **achieved** your goal, and is it time to create another one?

As your gratitude grows stronger, update your practice to tackle new challenges. Keep your practice interesting, change prompts, try a new method, or socialize it.

Workplace Applications

Everything you've learned about personal practice also applies to the workplace; only the stakes and scale are larger. Let's explore the workplace version of Goal, Plan, Do, which operates on a larger scale. The impact and potential backlash can be greater if not executed well. Workplace gratitude is a project and should be managed as one.

Workplace goals might be:
- Creating a culture of engagement
- Solving a specific challenge (toxic positivity, negativity)
- Clarifying why the business exists and aligning it
- Showing why your customers should care

Workplace planning tips:
- Ensure that there is a clear sponsor and senior leadership support
- Use surveys and interviews to identify toxic behaviors or beliefs
- Treat workplace gratitude initiatives like programs and projects with timelines and deliverables

Examples:
- Projects & Programs: Integrate gratitude into vision, scope, or requirements
- Processes: Embed gratitude into performance reviews, recognition, and rewards
- Technology & Tools: Track and measure gratitude through existing or new systems

Whether it's an online tool, an app, a dashboard, or an already existing and classic known tool, it is possible to adapt and integrate gratitude into it. Since early on, writing long-winded, over-fifty-page product requirements and plans, I included measurements for team positivity, without realizing what I was truly doing was incorporating ongoing learning, growth of positivity, and gratitude. A simple example is that a must-have after each significant milestone is to have a type of team celebration and reward. The duration between celebrations must be shorter than a month.

Here's another example of the class project management stakeholder matrix, revised to focus on creating positive teams and relationships. I use this tool with leaders today. I call it a PPP Matrix (Positive, Proactive, Professional). You rate each stakeholder on a scale of 1-10 in each category, then total the scores. You'll immediately see the relationships that need the most attention.

Management Tool Example (PPP Matrix)

Stakeholder	Positive	Proactive	Professional	Total
Manager	5	4	9	18
Sponsors	8	6	9	23
Tech Leader	9	9	5	23
Customer A	7	3	10	20
Team A	8	8	8	24
Team B	6	7	9	22
IT Support	5	4	7	16
Legal	7	5	9	21
Marketing	4	7	8	19

Use the totals to identify where to focus on improving relationships. Each stakeholder is an opportunity to help you succeed or fail at your project.

Measuring Gratitude in Workplaces

Workplaces and teams require additional and distinct criteria as part of their gratitude baseline to measure gratitude. Examples of what could be measured in the baseline are: stress level, turnover rates, positivity, or recognition and celebrations.

One common measure used in workplaces is engagement. Here are some real examples of surveys and what they measure to consider for what to include in your workplace gratitude baseline:

- **Gallup Q12 Employee Engagement Survey:** includes items like, *"In the last seven days, I have received recognition or praise for doing good work."*
- **Great Place to Work® Trust Index Survey:** measures respect, fairness, and pride, indicators of a positive, appreciative culture.
- **Psychological Safety Index (Amy Edmondson):** measures whether employees feel safe to express themselves.
- **Positive Organizational Behavior (POB) Metrics:** includes gratitude alongside hope, optimism, and resilience.

Company B Corporation (B Corp) Assessment
Another good source of measurements for the workplace is found in the questions used to award a company the designation of a B Corp. A B Corp is a certified for-profit business that is a purpose-driven entity that prioritizes making a positive difference in the world, whether through its products, services, or operations.

Certified B Corps go through an assessment (B Impact Assessment) that includes questions about positivity in the workplace:

- Do you have regular employee satisfaction surveys?
- What percentage of your workforce receives recognition awards or bonuses?
- Do you track voluntary turnover and act on feedback?
- Do you offer wellness programs or mental health resources?

B Corp certification signals that a company actively:

- Builds a positive workplace
- Recognizes and appreciates employees
- Supports well-being, inclusion, and fairness

This matters because:

- It reduces turnover
- Strengthens customer loyalty
- Increases resilience in downturns
- Encourages long-term orientation

Final Thoughts

Gratitude for leaders and workplaces must be normalized and continually reinforced to prevent erosion in the workplace. It requires intentional focus and accountability to strengthen. Like a muscle, it will weaken if not exercised, and it will plateau if you don't stretch it.

With a clear 'Why,' a thoughtful Plan, and consistent action, gratitude becomes more than a habit; it becomes a program, projects, and processes that ensure gratitude and all its benefits are infused into you and your workplace culture.

Gratitude Practice Framework Takeaways

- Gratitude thrives when you measure and manage it intentionally.
- Your practice should fit your life and goals. There's no single correct method, and it changes over time.
- There are three steps in the methodology for a gratitude strengthening project: Goal (Why) → Plan (What, How, When) → Do (Act and Adjust)
- Consistently reflect and adjust as needed.
- Workplace gratitude should be measured and treated like a real project for success.
- Build checkpoints into your practice and workplace systems.
- Start now, even if only for 30 seconds, and gratitude will improve your day.

Reflection Questions

1. What are your Why, Purpose, Vision, and specific gratitude goals?

2. What is your plan for practice? How will you measure success?

3. What is needed in your workplace for Goal, Plan, Do?

Chapter 20
Kitchen Sink Challenges

Everything is as it should be.
~ Trenton Lee Stewart, The Mysterious Benedict
Society

This chapter begins with one of my favorite reminders: whatever level of gratitude you have right now is as it should be. You are not behind. You are not doing it "wrong." There's no gold star for gratitude, no hidden scoreboard, no universal definition you must achieve.

What follows are more challenges and possible solutions; some of the challenges were not covered earlier. New challenges keep emerging, so I offer an online site that I will continually update and expand. See the QR code and links at the end of the chapter for worksheets and updates.

The sky is the limit in how you can practice gratitude. What follows is a menu of challenges and possibilities, the kitchen sink, or the buffet of challenges and solutions. These are from personal and leadership gratitude journeys, mine and others.

What's next is an invitation to reflect, explore, and experiment. Take what you need, might try, and ignore the rest.

Challenge: Boredom with Gratitude

Over time, even something as powerful as gratitude can feel stale.

My mother used to say, "Only bored people get bored." Thanks, Mom. I hear her voice in my head whenever I feel that creeping sense of sameness in my gratitude practice. After 20+ years of daily journaling, I've noticed moments when it feels repetitive.

There are only so many ways to say you're thankful for your health, your family, your job, or your morning coffee. When boredom sets in, you might be tempted to drop your practice altogether. Instead, see boredom as an invitation to get creative. Here are some things you can try.

Active gratitude, not passive. Instead of writing, "I'm grateful for my pet," try, "I'm grateful that I was able to buy food and feed my pet organic food today."

Get curious. Ask yourself new questions. "What am I overlooking?" "What small, ordinary thing made today easier?"

Play with it. Build gratitude into a game or playful ritual. Create a Gratitude Jar, each day drop in a note of thanks and watch the jar fill over time. Or build a points system for yourself. How many moments of gratitude can you collect in a day?

Gamify it. Use apps or trackers to make gratitude fun. Set challenges: "Find 10 new things to be grateful for before lunch." Or try toys or counters, like moving beads from one jar to another every time you notice something good.

Think like a toddler; speak like a professional. Toddlers are naturally curious, endlessly noticing and delighting in the small things. Channel that energy. Look around with fresh eyes. Then, when sharing gratitude with others, use thoughtful, professional language that matches your context.

Experiment. Ask friends for ideas. Search online. Ask AI for prompts. Challenge yourself to list 100 ways to express gratitude or invent your own.

Boredom isn't a sign that gratitude isn't working. It's a sign that your practice is ready to evolve.

Challenge: Too Busy, No Time

"I'm stressed, I'm overwhelmed, and there is no way I can find five extra minutes in my day."

Sound familiar? You are not alone. Life moves fast, and when we're juggling demands, gratitude can feel like a luxury we can't afford.

The irony is that the stronger your gratitude practice becomes, the less stressed and overwhelmed you will feel. Gratitude doesn't take time; it creates time by shifting your focus, calming your nervous system, and opening your mind to solutions.

You don't have to start big. Begin small. Here's a progressive menu of practices you can fit into even the busiest schedule:

30 Seconds – Shift to Gratitude.

When you feel stress creeping in, pause for half a minute. Take a deep breath and intentionally think of one thing, just one, that you're grateful for in that exact moment. A sip of water. A smile from someone. The fact that you're breathing.

1 Minute - Ask and Listen.

Turn to someone near you, at home, at work, or even on a call, and ask, "What's one thing you're grateful for today?" Then listen. You'll not only connect with them, but you'll feel your own gratitude grow.

2 Minutes – Watch a Ted Lasso Clip.
Yes, really. Queue up a short clip of Ted Lasso facing a challenge with humor and optimism. In two minutes, you'll witness gratitude in action. My favorite - Season 2, Episode 5, when he reminds his team, "Fairy tales don't end at the dark forest."

5 Minutes – Do a Quick Gratitude Journal Page.
Grab a notebook, a sticky note, or your phone. Set a timer for five minutes and list everything that comes to mind. Don't overthink. Let it flow. Even on a hectic day, you'll be surprised by how much you have to write.

Try combining these with activities you already do, while brushing your teeth, waiting, standing in line, or on hold. Tiny pockets of time add up to a powerful practice.

Remember, gratitude isn't about finding hours; it's about finding moments. Every second you choose gratitude is a second that strengthens gratitude.

Challenge: What do I do to start my practice?
Gratitude is like a muscle. Muscle strength varies from person to person, and gratitude can be strengthened or weakened over time. Your gratitude strength might shift throughout the day, depending on your conscious and unconscious responses, physically,

mentally, and emotionally, to whatever's happening around you.

The three main components of strong gratitude muscles are consistency, depth, and the ability to shift quickly back to gratitude. Negative conditions, ongoing stress, uncertainty, or big changes will test the strength of your gratitude.

Measure and Label

Start by labeling and identifying how strong your gratitude feels right now. Create a gratitude baseline and date it. Write down where you feel solid and where you struggle. Then, pick the lowest-scoring area and apply a solution. Keep track of your growth over time.

Find "I'm not grateful" triggers

Identify situations that cause you not to feel grateful. Keep a log or note them. For example, you might notice frustration whenever someone uses 'that' tone, says 'that' phrase, or stays silent when you wish they'd speak up. Get curious about why those behaviors bother you and why they might be happening. Look for something about that person or situation you can appreciate, even if it's small. Explore your mindset and beliefs.

Use All Senses

Identify something or someone you're already grateful for and pause. Reflect on why. Then dig deeper and ask yourself repeatedly: "What else am I grateful for here?" Let new insights surface slowly. Write them down. Use all your senses: see, feel, touch, hear, and taste as appropriate. Strengthening your emotional intelligence, compassion, and empathy will naturally increase depth.

Challenge: Being grateful for difficult situations

Discernment is seeing the whole picture and finding something to be grateful for even in difficult circumstances. A leader was heading into a meeting the next day to address major funding cuts and the possibility of significant layoffs. "What could I possibly be grateful for?" she asked our small group after I spoke to the group about gratitude. I replied sincerely: "You are alive. You have a job today." The group went silent. So, I shifted into teacher mode and shared the story of Elie Wiesel, Holocaust survivor, author of *Night*, and Nobel Peace Prize winner, who once said that while in a concentration camp, he was grateful for food. When we're faced with overwhelming circumstances, we don't need to fake gratitude; we can start from the bottom and work our way up, finding common ground before tackling the hard stuff.

Discernment doesn't mean agreement or approval. It's the ability to hold opposites: to see the harm and still find something worth appreciating.

Try this:
Keep asking yourself what you might be grateful for about a person or situation that challenges you. Start with the most basic. If nothing comes to mind, ask someone else what they see.

Challenge: What's my preferred way to practice gratitude?

Here are various ways people practice gratitude for you to try. There is no "right" way. It's finding what works for you.

Write It
- Use a paper journal, an app, or a dedicated gratitude journal.
- Challenge yourself to list 100 or even 1,000 things you are grateful for.
- Pick one thing and explore it deeply on both a micro and macro level.
- Reflect on what choices you made today that you are grateful for and how you contributed.
- Keep a gratitude box or jar that you fill daily with notes.
- Create a notebook of people you're grateful for and write them letters.

- Start a morning texting group and share daily gratitude with your friends.

Say It Out Loud - To yourself, to strangers, to friends, to family, just say it.

See It
- Look for gratitude and create visual cues in your environment.
- Hang images or use screen savers that remind you of gratitude.
- Create a gratitude board on social media or bookmark inspiring things you find on the internet.
- Build an album (digital or physical) of things you're grateful for.
- Collect quotes or memes that make you smile.

Story It - Find a person or a story that inspires you. Feel the story, watch the story, and let it move you.

Reframe Your Story - Take a personal story and rewrite it, turning all the negatives into positives.

Touch It - Find physical sensations that elevate your feel-good chemicals, such as a pet's fur, a soft stone, or a textured surface.

Count It and Game It - How often each day do you express gratitude or say, "Thank you"? How many people are you grateful for, and do they know it?

Watch It - A sunset, a giggling baby, funny pet videos, a favorite movie, or an inspiring TED Talk. Stop, Look, and Go to Shift to Gratitude TED Talk, from Br. David Steindl-Rast: Want to be happy? Be grateful | TED Talk

Listen to It - Music or sounds that instantly make you feel grateful. Here's my Gratitude Gap Closer playlist on Spotify: https://open.spotify.com/playlist/22tVw0PIEz u5zkrlloV1ET?si=16jig3mSRX6XEVjVXj_yRw

Read It - Inspiring stories, books, Substack, Medium, or blogs.

Move to It - Dance, walk, run, or ramble in nature.

Be Mindful - Be 100% present. Stop thinking about the past or future, mindfulness practices, meditation, prayer, or movement all help.

Meditate - Learn to quiet your mind. Join a group, take a course, go on a retreat, or try apps like Calm or Insight Timer.

Compassion - Build compassion for yourself and others. Dr. Kristin Neff's workbook on Self-

Compassion is excellent. Check out her courses, books, and community.

Volunteer and Give - Find a cause you care about and offer your time regularly or occasionally, in person or virtually.

Language It - Experiment with your words. Try removing "no," "never," and "but" from your vocabulary.

Do Without - Appreciate something by going without it, coffee, water, or something else. Absence often deepens appreciation.

Socialize It - Start an in-person or online gratitude group. Challenge each other to share specific gratitude regularly.

Book Club - Join or start a book club where gratitude is always on the agenda.
Join me in my monthly Leadership GEMS for leadership topics paired with gratitude insights. www.starleadership.com/monthly-leadership-gems

One-Day Experiment - For one day, find something about every person you encounter that you're truly grateful for and tell them.

Create or Participate in a Gratitude Challenge - Here's a sample 8-day challenge based on the work in this book, to try.

Day #1 - **Find** your Gratitude Purpose - Why do you want to strengthen your gratitude? See Chapter 6.

Day #2 - **Define and Declare** Your Gratitude Definition. What does gratitude mean to you? Write it down and tell someone. See Chapter 10.

Day #3 - **Measure** Gratitude. Create your gratitude baseline and date it. Chapter 7

Day #4 - **Try Active** Gratitude, Not Passive. What are you grateful for that you did recently? (example: I am grateful I chose to attend this event)

Day #5 - Be Grateful for **360 Degrees** of One Thing. Find all the pre-, post-, next, and future that went into this one thing to be thankful for. (water: plumbing, pumping stations, testers, nature)

Day #6 - Start with **Common Ground**. Find someone you are not grateful for and find something in common with them. (Verbalize when there is conflict)

Day #7 - **Hold One Opposite**. Pick one negative emotion and, at the same time, be grateful. (anger and grateful)

Day #8 – Find an **Integration** Point. Pick something you do regularly and integrate gratitude into it. (teeth brushing, coffee)

Challenge: I slip out of gratitude. What do I do?
Shift - Learn and apply the three-step shift to gratitude as described in Chapter 11.

Time Limits - During my divorce, I didn't know how to grieve or feel anger. I carried so much sadness that I'd burst into tears at odd moments. I created a window of negativity: a 15-minute timer where I sat with betrayal, anger, guilt, regret, and grief. After a year, I noticed I had worked through most of it and was productive and happy again. That process helped me heal.

It Sucks List - Keep a list of things, people, or situations that you dislike. See how long you can stay with the negative before returning to gratitude. This helps you get clear and become aware so that you can dig deeper and reframe it, ignore it, or take action.

Teach Gratitude Skills – To get better at something, to understand it deeply, to understand where other people are, and where they might need to go, consider teaching (not telling, not preaching) gratitude. By teaching, researching, and being grateful, it naturally helps to shift you to being more grateful. Develop a gratitude workshop for your team. See the extra resources we have included in the QR code.

Daily Reminders - Create visible daily reminders of habits and behaviors that strengthen your gratitude muscle. Here's a daily reminders list we made for leaders: https://starleadership.com/gratitude-daily-reminders/

Maintain a High Positive-to-Negative Ratio - High-performing teams often aim for around 5 to 6 positive comments for every negative one. The exact number is debated, but the principle stands: keep affirmations high.

Have someone count gratitude sentiments, measure them, and include them as your team's baseline; gamify this! Warning: Ensure it's genuine gratitude.

Challenge: How to strengthen workplace gratitude?
Gratitude at the leadership level is not about being perfect or relentlessly positive. It's about creating an environment where people feel seen, valued, and inspired to contribute their best work. With these tools, you can model gratitude, teach it, and embed it into your culture. When you do, you'll close the gratitude gap not just for yourself but for everyone you lead.

Meetings

- Start with laughter; a one-minute clip of smiling babies can set a positive tone.
- Share culturally appropriate TV or movie clips before tackling tough topics.

Environment

Create a workspace, physical or virtual, that fosters gratitude. Use visuals, colors, music, and stories. Play upbeat music when appropriate.

Stories

Collect and share gratitude stories. They tell us who we are and guide our practices. We can tell the story to highlight the gratitude or the negative and unethical; what we focus on will propagate. Here's a true example from a company I worked with.

An executive was caught stealing from the company. Two organizations in the same company created very different stories. One leader, known for gratitude, framed it as a cautionary tale and strengthened security. The other leader's group speculated on how to steal without getting caught. One situation, the same, yet two cultures, gratitude changed the narrative and was associated with the more productive organization.

Another company shares gratitude stories on monitors throughout their offices and during agile scrum stand-ups. It took effort to start, but it soon became an engaging habit.

Summary

Gratitude is not about achieving perfection; it's about practice and growth. Each challenge you face, whether boredom, busyness, or the setbacks of real life, is not a barrier but an invitation to strengthen your gratitude muscles. The menu of solutions here is not meant to overwhelm you, but to remind you that you already have what you need to keep growing.

If you recognize yourself or your workplace in these challenges, know you're not alone. Each challenge is simply a doorway, an invitation to explore a new aspect of gratitude. You don't have to fix everything at once. Choose one, try a suggestion, and reflect. Let yourself experiment and grow. And wherever you are, remember, everything is as it should be.

The goal of the book is to recognize the challenges and take action to strengthen your gratitude foundation, whether by being more consistent, deepening your appreciation, or shifting your perspective. The challenge is to keep looking and to find what works for you and your workplace. Focus on what activates the feeling of gratitude as authentically and quickly as possible.

For me, ocean waves instantly calm me. My mind and body relax, and I feel a sense of gratitude. For you, it might be a particular song, a favorite painting, or the smell of your morning coffee. Pay attention to what sparks gratitude in you and create and build on that. As a leader, know that what sparks gratitude for you might not for someone else.

When you bring gratitude into your leadership, you not only shift your own perspective, you create workplaces where people feel seen, valued, and inspired to contribute their best. And when that happens, you are already closing the Gratitude Gap.

Additional Resources

This QR Code takes you to a place where you'll find additional worksheets, lists, challenges, and solutions. It includes live links for the references section. www.starleadership.com/thegratitudegap-bookresources

Chapter 21
Closing the Gratitude Gap

Yesterday I was so clever, so I wanted to change the world. Today I am wise, so I am changing myself.
~ Rumi

We began this journey by naming the Gratitude Gap: the space between knowing gratitude matters and consistently living and strengthening it. Along the way, you learned the Three Gratitude Truths that everything is better with gratitude, that it is a foundational leadership skill, and that it is both simple and challenging. These truths are more than concepts; they serve as a compass for leaders.

Gratitude is not fluff or a motivational slogan. It is a practice, a discipline, and a way of showing up even when the pressure mounts. The science confirms its power: gratitude strengthens the mind, steadies emotions, and deepens connection. The stories reveal impacts: leaders who express gratitude create workplaces where people feel valued, resilient, and inspired. Which, in turn, builds trust and engagement, creating better, more sustainable, successful results. The challenges we explored show gratitude's complexity. Genuine gratitude is never forced, faked, or transactional. It expects nothing in return. And it can be fast and straightforward to grow. Sometimes it's hard to see our challenges.

Leadership will always be tested by crisis, by change, by uncertainty. Gratitude doesn't erase those realities; it is always available and builds a foundation for you to face them with clarity and humanity. It helps you see opportunity in change, maintain trust when the ground shifts, and anchor yourself and others in what truly matters. Gratitude does not make you a perfect leader; it makes you a more human one.

Now the work is yours. Define gratitude clearly for yourself and your team. Measure it. Build your baseline. Make it strong by practicing it daily in your decisions, your meetings, and your conversations. Let it drip steadily into your leadership until it becomes second nature.

When you close the Gratitude Gap, you do more than improve performance; you transform workplaces into places of trust, purpose, and possibility. You become the kind of leader the world needs: effective, human, and deeply grateful.

Closing the Gratitude Gap

The future of leadership will not be defined by titles, strategies, or even technology; it will be defined by human leaders who practice gratitude. Close the gap, and you won't just change how you lead; you'll change what leadership means. The Gratitude Gap is real, and so is your power to close it.

Now is the time for leaders to embody their humanity, call it forth in others, and lead with gratitude, because that is how we change the world.

In Gratitude,
Star

Gratitude Leadership Questions

I formally interviewed over thirty leaders. To find people to speak with, I often started by asking, *"Who do you know that you would consider a grateful leader?"*

For this book, I recorded each interview and worked from the transcripts to create monthly blog posts. Every blog post was reviewed and approved by the person I interviewed. Their voices and stories are woven throughout these pages. Some stories didn't make it into the blog but found a home here instead. In a few cases, names have been changed, sometimes at their request, and sometimes by my own judgment.

I asked each person the same set of core questions, yet I also allowed the conversation to flow naturally. I followed their energy, their passion, and the moments where gratitude showed up most vividly. I stayed quiet about my own views on gratitude until each interview was complete, so their words could lead the way.

Below are the questions I used for the formal, recorded interviews:

1. Can you give me a little background on yourself? What or who do you identify with? (birth, religion, age range, group, physical location, identity with, profession)?
2. What do you believe about gratitude?
3. How do you define gratitude?
4. Do you have any regular gratitude practices, and what are they?
5. How grateful do you see yourself as on a scale from 1–10? (10 is an expert of gratitude)
6. What impact has gratitude made in your life?
7. How do you use gratitude at work?
8. What challenges have you had with gratitude?
9. What challenges have you noticed in others about gratitude?
10. How do you see other people use gratitude at work?
11. What do you see as the impact of gratitude at work?
12. Anything else you want to share about gratitude?

Additionally, I conducted a public gratitude survey using SurveyMonkey as the tool, which I reported on in April 2023. A little less than fifty people responded. A summary of the results of the survey are here:
www.starleadership.com/gratitude-challenge-must-practice/

Gratitude and Thank You

Let us rise up and be thankful, for if we didn't learn a lot today, at least we learned a little. And if we didn't learn a little, at least we didn't get sick. And if we got sick, at least we didn't die. So, let us all be thankful.
 ~ Buddha

I have miles to go before I finish expressing all the gratitude I feel. This book has truly been a lifetime in the making. It surprised me how it turned out; it is not what I first imagined. Over time, it became much more about the generous, thoughtful people around me and about me and the lessons we've discovered together.

The path of gratitude is long and endless. These words and ideas have been alive in me for more than seven years and represent a lifetime. What you're holding is an accumulation of what I've learned, what I've witnessed firsthand, and what I've researched about gratitude. I'm certain I've left someone out or made mistakes along the way, and for that, I sincerely apologize. Through the lens of gratitude, mistakes aren't failures; they are lessons waiting to be learned. If you notice a lesson I still need to learn, please let me know.

I'm deeply grateful to every person who didn't run away when I started talking about gratitude, who listened patiently and answered my seemingly endless, nuanced questions.

To my husband, Steve, your love of non-fiction and your insights helped me make this book more engaging and less technical.

To Donna Howard, your artwork has inspired me for years and graces the walls of my home. Never did I imagine I would see it on the cover of this book. Thank you for that gift.

To my sister Lee, my daughter-in-law Katie, and all those brave enough to tell me when something didn't make sense, thank you. To my family, Mike, Kevin, Ryan, Cam, and Ava, I love you all deeply and appreciate you more than words can ever express.

To my NH ladies' mastermind group, Pam Richardson, Tara Whitney, and Sandra Long, you wouldn't let me give up. Maybe you were tired of hearing me talk about it, but your insistence kept me going.

To Carole, thank you for your honesty, your unflinching feedback, and for helping me untangle and organize the challenges of gratitude.

To Gwen, your steady phone calls and your offers of help pushed me to rethink the structure and outline of this book. I'm grateful beyond measure.

To my early readers: Ned, Lee, Steve, Margo, Katie, Larry, Don, Brian, Kathleen, Wendy, Gail, Chris, and John, thank you for your time and thoughtful comments.

To my editors, Nancy Struckman and Lisa J Jackson, you refined my words with care and precision.

To Emily Aborn, a talented copywriter and podcaster, thank you for your gifts and encouragement.

To my excellent assistants, Andrea, Meredith, and LeAnn E, thank you for supporting me in countless ways.

To the team at 100 Covers, thank you for creating a cover that captures the spirit of this book using Donna's artwork.

To all the incredible people and organizations that invited me to bring gratitude into their workplaces, you gave me a living laboratory in which to test these ideas. A special thank you to Amy at Weston & Sampson, who hired me specifically for my focus on gratitude. Just before this book went to print, we completed our coaching together and offered these words that feel like the very heart of what I wish for every reader:

"Star's practice is rooted in gratitude, which is essential to me to be kind and express gratitude. I want to be a positive-minded leader. The result is that I am now a more confident and comfortable leader. I'm working at a higher level and a sounding board for peers and others. I'm getting better business results through collaboration and successful conflict management. I'm happier and leading from a much more positive place."

To the people at NEXX, TEL, UKG, Toyota, the Commonwealth of Massachusetts, Casey Hall Associates, NASA, Weston & Sampson, North Shore Community College, and Boston University, thank you for trusting me with your teams and your learning journeys.

At Boston University, I am especially grateful to Vijay Kanbar, who took a chance on me, a subject-matter expert without a fancy formal degree, by inviting me to teach a graduate-level course where I infused gratitude and positive leadership into project management. To my mentor, Virginia Greiman at Boston University, who sadly passed while I was writing this book. I wish I had interviewed her. She was the ultimate professional and showed me how gratitude can be practiced even with the most challenging students and administrators.

I am deeply thankful to everyone who completed the gratitude survey, and to every leader who shared their gratitude stories with me during interviews.

This is only a short list of the multitude of people I hold in my heart. It takes a village to write a book and breathe life into it. To everyone named here and to those I've unintentionally left out, you are part of this journey.

From the depths of my heart: **thank you.**
Star xo

Connect with Star

Gratitude enables us to see our reality and accept it as a gift. With the gift of gratitude, we are more capable of knowing and creating the reality of our vision.
~ Star Sargent Dargin

Over the years, I've discovered that the leaders who create the most impact are not necessarily the ones with the longest résumés or the largest teams. They are the ones who embrace gratitude as a skill, a lens, and a daily practice. They are the ones who see connections others might miss and create workplaces where people feel seen, valued, trusted, and inspired.

My work and this book is built on three Gratitude Truths that I teach and try to live every day:

Truth #1 - Everything is better with gratitude.
Gratitude amplifies performance, deepens relationships, and creates resilience in times of change and challenge. When you work with me, you'll discover practical ways to integrate gratitude into your leadership habits to receive the many physical, mental, and social benefits of gratitude that create sustainable, positive, and longer-lasting results.

Truth #2: Gratitude is a leadership skill.
Gratitude is not fluff or an add-on or a "soft skill"; it's a foundational competency that strengthens decision-making, improves team dynamics, and unlocks human potential. Through my coaching and workshops, I help leaders of all levels turn gratitude from a vague ideal into a concrete, measurable leadership tool.

Truth #3: Gratitude is both easy and challenging.
The concept is simple, yet the practice requires courage, consistency, and curiosity. Together, we explore the challenges that get in the way: time pressures, cultural differences, fear of vulnerability, and build real solutions you can use immediately.

Work with Star
As CEO of **Star Leadership**, I've spent decades partnering with senior leaders and organizations to create cultures where gratitude is not just felt, it's practiced, measured, and woven into daily leadership.

Executive Leadership Coaching: Elevate Your Leadership by Strengthening Gratitude as a Strategic Skill in Conjunction with Other Critical Leadership Skills. Coaching supports faster skill and behavior growth, leading to a more effective and significant impact for the leader. It targets the top-performing, high-potential employees the company wants to invest in, who are ready to take on the work.

Keynotes and Speaking: Bring your teams and organizations into the conversation with interactive sessions on gratitude and leading.

My clients include Fortune 50 companies, educational institutions, government agencies, and mission-driven organizations—places where leaders are committed to shaping workplaces that are both high-performing and deeply human.

Connect with Star
Let's stay in touch and keep growing together.
www.starleadership.com
LinkedIn – Star Leadership

Sign up for my newsletter:
www.starleadership.com/newsletter
When you join, you'll receive resources to support your gratitude journey.

Gratitude isn't a one-time act; it's a lifelong practice that evolves as you do.

I look forward to walking this path with you. Let's connect and lead with gratitude together.

References for Each Chapter

Gratitude is a powerful catalyst for happiness. It's the spark that lights a fire of joy in your soul. ~ Amy Collette

To keep this book readable, accessible, and up-to-date in print, the full list of references is available online, along with additional resources to support the ideas and practices in this book. You can access the complete reference list and resources at **https://starleadership.com/thegratitudegap-references/** or by scanning the QR code provided.